Called to Preach
Now What?

Roy W. Harris

Dedications

(Listed chronologically in the order they impacted my life beginning in 1969)

Reverend Ed Hargis, my father in the ministry who saw the preacher in me before I saw it myself: He gave me my first opportunity to preach and encouraged me in my early years of ministry.

Mrs. Laura Thigpen my Welch College Freshman Speech teacher who helped me learn the basics that served me well for over four decades of public speaking.

Reverend Jack Paramore who preached a message on commitment that God used to speak to my heart about entering the Gospel ministry.

Mr. Brack Brewer whom God used to provide me with my first resource outside the Bible to build many of my early sermons.

Mr. Ralph Hampton, my Welch College Homiletics teacher who taught the elements of sermons and how to put them together and preach them.

Members of Ahoskie Free Will Baptist Church, Ahoskie, North Carolina - my first pastorate - who were very kind and patient with me in my early years of preaching God's word. You will always hold a special place in my heart.

Members of Zephyr Hills Free Will Baptist Church, Asheville, North Carolina, who introduced me and purchased my first computer, revolutionizing my approach to sermon and teaching preparation.

Members of First Free Will Baptist Church, Savannah, Georgia, who allowed me to develop a number of sermon series that I have revised and continue to use.

Members of Cane Ridge Free Will Baptist Church, Nashville, Tennessee who honored me by allowing me to be your pastor two different times and stood with me during a very difficult time in my life.

Members of Lake View Fellowship, Bowling Green, Kentucky, who allowed me to preach to them over four decades, serving as their interim pastor on three different occasions.

Pastors and Leaders across East Africa who have allowed me to preach and teach them in over 20 Pastors and Leaders Training Conferences, as well as several Evangelistic Crusades.

Special thanks to *Dr. Brenda Williams* my editor. Her hard work, knowledge, skill and attention to detail elevated this book to a much higher level.

Contents

Introduction

When I arrived at home with my parents after completing my freshman year at Welch College, I didn't realize it, but this would be my last summer at home. I would be married and on my own by the next summer.

I had answered God's call to preach his word seven months before and had preached my first sermon four months earlier during Christmas break at my home church in Anderson, Indiana. I hadn't received any training on how to write and prepare sermons, but God blessed and we saw three people make commitments to Christ during the invitation. However, I realized while preparing my first sermon that I had much to learn.

My father mentioned that a man in our church named Brack Brewer wanted to see me. Dad called Brack and made arrangements for us to stop by a few days later.

I admired Brack and was curious as to why he wanted to see me. He told me he had something for me. He and his wife, Allie, lived across the street from Anderson College. There had been a fire in one of the buildings at the college earlier, and the college demolished the building so it could be replaced. Debris was scattered over the area.

Brack noticed a small, light blue spiral-bound booklet approximately four inches wide and about nine inches long lying on the ground. It had apparently fallen from a truck hauling away debris.

He picked up the booklet. It was singed on one corner from the fire and smelled of smoke. The print on the cover indicated it was a book of simple sermon outlines. Brack had immediately thought of me and felt impressed by the Lord to give me the booklet. He handed me the little book, and I thanked him for his kindness and generosity.

I thumbed through the notebook, and I could feel my heart leap within. It was filled with short bare-bones sermon outlines, about three to a page. Each outline contained a sermon title, Bible text reference, and three or four points.

Here is an example:

A Better Church Begins With Me
1 Corinthians 12:20-26

1. If you want the church to be better, realize that you are important.
2. If you want the Church to be better, you must do something for it.
3. If you want the church to be better, you must invite others to share its blessings.

The little book contained approximately 150 short outlines and became my main source, outside the Bible, for developing my sermons.

I realized early in my young preaching ministry that the more *sermon preparation tools* I could lay my hands on, the easier and more effective my sermons would become.

I have a love and appreciation for young preachers. I've spent much of my life mentoring young men for service in God's kingdom. This, in part, is why this book was written. I also want young preachers to be effective and not to flounder as they *rightly divide the truth* and proclaim God's word.

The pages that follow are an effort to equip, encourage, and empower young preachers with the *basic sermon preparation tools* to become the best preachers possible.

Called to Preach

I was well into the second month of my freshman year at Free Will Baptist Bible College (now called Welch College.) I was sitting at my desk in Room 210 of Goen Hall reading my Bible. Raymond, my college roommate, was studying at the library, and I was enjoying some quiet time with the Lord.

Jack Paramore had preached a message earlier urging us to seek God's perfect will for our lives. He impressed on us that the way to peace, contentment and happiness in life is to find God's will and do it.

The message took root deep in my heart. I went forward during the invitation at the end of the message, asking God to reveal to me what he wanted me to do with my life.

I promised God that night that I would be whatever he wanted me to be, do whatever he wanted me to do, and go wherever he wanted me to go. I surrendered the rest of my life, love, hope, and dreams to Christ and his plans for me.

The quietness of the room gave way to a strong

sense of God's presence. The word of God came alive with the still small voice of the Holy Spirit speaking from the pages of his Holy Scriptures.

My eyes moved down the page, carefully taking in each verse of the book of 1 Corinthians chapter nine. The apostle Paul says a great deal about preaching and the preacher in that chapter. The more I read, the more I understood what the voice of the Holy Spirit was softly saying to me: *You will be a preacher of my Word. This is what I want you to do.*

I dropped to my knees in front my chair, buried my face in my arms on the seat and prayed earnestly and fervently to the Lord. I felt so unworthy and wasn't sure I could do it, but I said yes to the Lord that night and promised, with his help, to preach his word.

I rose from my knees feeling the great peace of God overshadowing me. The moment was filled with a sense of excitement, satisfaction, and contentment. God had revealed the purpose for which he had created me. I was called to praise him and bring honor and glory to him by preaching his message of hope, help, and healing.

My first impulse was to let others know. I quickly made my way downstairs to the lobby of our dormitory. I told one of my close friends, Danny Thompson, of my decision and he announced to the lobby full of guys that I had just answered the call to preach. The lobby erupted with applause and several hardy Amens! A room full of young men laying hands on me, thanking God for his call on my life, and praying that he would use me in a mighty way followed this.

The Seriousness of the Call

God's call to preach his Gospel is a serious matter. We should understand the gravity of the call before we say yes.

As a minister, one's ultimate accountability for the sermon is not to the deacons, congregation, or alma mater, but to Christ. Christ calls and empowers us, and we will answer to him and undergo his examination. Romans 14:12 makes this very clear: *So then every one of us shall give account of himself to God.*

In his notes, Albert Barnes states this about preachers: *The preacher's character and conduct; his words and actions; his plans and purposes. in the fearful arraignment of that day, every work and purpose shall be brought forth, and tried by the unerring standard of justice. As we shall be called to so fearful an account with God, we should not be engaged in condemning our brethren, but should examine whether we are prepared to give up our account with joy, and not with grief.*

Preachers are held to a high standard, God's standard. We are called to accountability when we are called to preach. The apostle James cautions preachers: *My brethren, be not many masters, knowing that we shall receive the greater condemnation* (James 3:1).

Every believer will appear before the judgment seat of Christ. But the strictest, strongest, and severest judgment is reserved for preachers and teachers of the Word of God. We must remember that the call to preach is a serious matter. The call involves heavy responsibilities, divine accountability, and eternal consequences.

The Certainty of the Call

How can we know for sure that God has called us to preach?

A good indicator of the calling of God on one's life is a deep burning desire to preach his word, a desire that cannot be denied. The apostle Paul and the prophet Jeremiah experienced this desire.

Paul said in 1 Corinthians 9:16: *For if I preach the gospel, that gives me no ground for boasting. For necessity is laid upon me. Woe to me if I do not preach the gospel!* ESV Paul is saying that he was *compelled* or *driven* by an irresistible and undeniable compulsion to preach.

The Old Testament preacher Jeremiah felt the burden to preach so heavily that he could do nothing but preach. Note his words found in Jeremiah 20:8-9: *For whenever I speak, I cry out, I shout, violence and destruction! For the word of the Lord has become for me a reproach and derision all day long. If I say, I will not mention him, or speak any more in his name, there is in my heart as it were a burning fire shut up in my bones, and I am weary with holding it in, and I cannot."* ESV

Do you have that burning in your bones? Do you feel that you will literally explode if you do not proclaim the good news of the Gospel to others? Do you feel that, *Woe to me, if I do not preach,* 1 Corinthians 9:16 ESV. If you have that strong feeling that only God can give, that's one indicator that God has called you to preach.

Another indication of the call of God to preach

is the response by others to early messages. A positive response is a good indication that the preacher has the gift of teaching (διδασκαλίας pronounced *didaktikos,* original Greek word found in Ephesians 4:11.)

Every preacher must also be an effective teacher of God's Word. He must understand it, convey it clearly, and accurately apply it in personal ways to the hearers.

Responses by fellow ministers and church leaders are a third indication and good barometer of whether a man has the gift of preaching. The minister should possess the character and abilities, and should also meet the requirements outlined in 1 Timothy 3 and Titus 1. He should be examined and his call authenticated by his fellow preachers and church leaders.

The call of God to preach will be confirmed in many ways. More and more opportunities to preach will become available. Doors will close if it is not God's will for you to continue.

God is sovereign and in control of all things. Romans 8:28 reminds that: *We know that for those who love God all things work together for good, for those who are called according to his purpose.*

Every step in the process should only be taken after fervent prayer, a heart in tune with God's Holy Spirit, and living in sync with the Word of God. Only then can you know for certain that God has called you to preach.

Submission to the Call

John Newton, who is famous for writing the well known hymn Amazing Grace, once remarked: *None but He who made the world can make a Minister of the Gospel*.

Only God can call a true preacher. Only He can grant the preacher the gifts necessary for service. But the great promise of Scripture is that God does call preachers, and he gives these servants as gifts to the Church.

I'm convinced that God calls preachers. Only those whom he calls will be successful in the ministry. God calls, and we have the choice to say yes or no. I've heard preachers give testimonies about running from the call, sometimes for many years. We can choose to submit ourselves to the call of God or do as Moses did and say: *Lord send someone else*.

I experienced God's call and had to make a choice. The best decision I made in life was to say yes and submit to God's call to be his preacher.

I encourage you to do as 1 Peter 5:6 suggests: *Humble yourselves, therefore, under the mighty hand of God so that at the proper time he may exalt you* ESV. Submit to God's call and say, "*Yes, Lord.*" In his wisdom and sovereignty, he chose you. He knows you. He believes in you, and it's all about him. If you will humble yourself in submission to him, you will be amazed to see how he will exalt and raise you to heights you could never have imagined.

Say: *Yes Lord, I will preach your Word. I will be what you want me to be. I will go where you want me to go and I will do what you want me to do.* I assure you he will be with you every minute of every hour of every day.

The Office of Preacher

The Message

The message God wants proclaimed is simple. Jesus Christ paid the price for the sins of every person who has lived, is living, or will live. He died a cruel death on a cross and rose from the dead after three days.

Paul the apostle wrote in his first letter to the church at the city of Corinth, located in south central Greece, that the message he preached was simple; *we preach Christ and him crucified.* 1 Corinthians 1:23 ESV

Paul also describes how the message might be received. He tells us in 1 Corinthians 18:18-20 KJV that: *For the preaching of the cross is to them that perish foolishness; but unto us which are saved it is the power of God. For it is written, I will destroy the wisdom of the wise, and will bring to nothing the understanding of the prudent. Where is the wise? Where is the scribe? Where is the disputer of this world? Hath not God made foolish the wisdom of this world?*

The Method

God not only chose the message, but he also gives clear direction on his choice of how the message is to be shared.

The apostle Paul is straightforward in his pronouncement of the method God selected in 1 Corinthians 18:21 KJV: *For after that in the wisdom of God the world by wisdom knew not God, it pleased God by the foolishness of preaching to save them that believe.*

God chose preaching. What is preaching? The Merriam Webster Dictionary defines preaching as *delivering publically a sermon, earnestly advocating the acceptance or abandonment of an idea or course of action.*

The Bible contains many instances of preaching in the Old and New Testaments. Solomon was called the preacher in Ecclesiastes 1:1.

Isaiah the prophet proclaimed the good news to the poor in Isaiah 61:1: *The Spirit of the Sovereign LORD is on me, because the LORD has anointed me to proclaim* (preach) *good news to the poor. He has sent me to bind up the broken hearted, to proclaim freedom for the captives and release from darkness for the prisoners.* ESV

Jonah was instructed to proclaim a message of impending destruction to the inhabitants of the city of Nineveh in Jonah 3:2: *Go to the great city of Nineveh and proclaim* (preach) *to it the message I give you.* ESV

John the Baptist was the first preacher in the New Testament. Matthew 3:1 states: *In those days John the Baptist came, preaching in the wilderness of Judea.* ESV

Timothy was appointed to be a herald (preacher) to the Gentiles in 1 Timothy 2:7: *And for this purpose I was appointed a herald and an apostle—I am telling the truth, I am not lying—and a true and faithful teacher of the Gentiles.* ESV

Jesus fulfilled the prophesy of Isaiah 61:1 in Matthew 11:5 ESV when He said: *The blind receive sight, the lame walk, those who have leprosy are cleansed, the deaf hear, the dead are raised, and the good news is proclaimed (preached) to the poor.*

The Messenger

God gave the message. He chose the way it would be delivered and selected individuals who would proclaim that message to his creation. God chose the preacher to share the message of Christ and him crucified.

Romans 10:14-15 ESV states: *How then will they call on him in whom they have not believed? And how are they to believe in him of whom they have never heard? How are they to hear without someone preaching? And how are they to preach unless they are sent?*

The apostle Paul wrote in his letter to the church at Rome that people could not believe in Christ or call on him unless they heard about him. They would not be able to hear about Christ unless others told them. Those others would be preachers.

God chose to use preachers as his spokesmen to proclaim the good news of the Gospel. Preachers are the messengers, using God's method of preaching to proclaim the message of the Gospel. The office of preacher is a special calling that comes directly from God himself. Preachers bring messages of hope and peace, but sometimes of sorrow and destruction. They must proclaim the truth of the Word of God.

Paul tells us in Romans 10:15 that God holds preachers in high esteem: *As it is written, how beautiful are the feet of those who preach the good news.* ESV

The sacred office of preacher is of paramount importance in the Kingdom of God. The preacher plays a vital and essential role in the communication of the Gospel of Jesus Christ to a desperate world. The preacher *stands in the gap* and *makes up the hedge*, gathering the sheep of God's pasture and guiding the flock to shelter in all of life's storms.

The Command to Prepare

The call to preach is joined closely with the command to prepare. The Bible is filled with examples of the need for study, training, preparation, and education. The Old Testament model began with training by parents in the home, and there is no shortage of admonition to prepare in the New Testament.

Why should we prepare?

Why should we prepare to preach? It is because we are instructed to do so. Paul tells Timothy that he must study/prepare if he is to be an effective preacher. Notice what the apostle Paul instructed the young preacher Timothy to do in 2 Timothy 2:15: *Study to show thyself approved unto God, a workman that needeth not to be ashamed, rightly dividing the word of truth. KJV*

The original word for study that Paul uses in this verse is the Greek word σπούδασον. It literally means, to study, make haste, and be diligent. Paul instructed

Timothy to be conscientious in the way he handled the Word of God, knowing that he would receive God's approval or disapproval.

Each time we stand to proclaim God's Word, we should remember that God himself is looking at our hearts, listening to each word we speak, and recording the entire sermon for eternity. We must do our best to be as prepared as possible.

We will stand before God one day and be accountable for our ministries including each sermon we preach. We want Christ's approval and to hear him say; *Well done.* We do not want to hang our heads in shame hearing God's sad words of disapproval.

The original Greek word for rightly dividing, ὀρθοτομοῦντα, literally means to cut straight. By rightly dividing the word of truth, or making sure that we cut it on the line with each message we preach, we can be assured of receiving God's approval.

How can we rightly divide the word of truth? The answer is found in the first part of 2 Timothy 2:15: (my paraphrase) *by studying and being well prepared each time we preach so we won't embarrass ourselves in front of God the one we seek to please.*

How should we prepare?

Heart Preparation – Becoming effective preachers begins with living clean lives. Our lives must be free from known sin with heartfelt desire to live according to God's directions found in his Word.

The Bible says a great deal about keeping our vessels (bodies) clean and free from sin. 2 Timothy 2:20-22: *Now in a great house there are not only vessels of gold and silver but also of wood and clay, some for honorable use, some for dishonorable. Therefore, if anyone cleanses himself from what is dishonorable, he will be a vessel for honorable use, set apart as holy, useful to the master of the house, ready for every good work. So flee youthful passions and pursue righteousness, faith, love, and peace, along with those who call on the Lord from a pure heart.* ESV

We will not be effective in the ministry as a whole and preaching in particular if we are not clean and living holy lives above reproach. God cannot and will not use a *dirty vessel.*

Learn the Scriptures – The key to keeping our vessels clean and pure is the cleansing power of God's Word. The Holy Spirit uses the Word of God to warn us of impending actions that could result in sinning against God. We should learn the Scriptures and make them part of who we are as preachers.

The Psalmist said in Psalm 119:11: *I have stored up your Word in my heart, that I might not sin against you.* ESV We store up the Word of God by reading, meditating and memorizing it.

We must possess and be possessed by the Word of God if we are to be effective in proclaiming that Word to others. We should read the Word of God each day and allow the Holy Spirit to help it take root in our hearts.

We should be so familiar with the Word that the situations of life we encounter will trigger recall of the guiding light of the Word for each situation. This will also carry over into our preaching. The Holy Spirit uses the recall of the Word of God at appropriate and crucial points in each message we preach.

This is where the power of our preaching is felt by the hearers. If we want to preach with power and see results, then we must begin with a growing familiarity and understanding of God's Word.

Prepare Intellectually – Recognize that your preaching will be shallow and limited if you do not prepare your mind. Sharing the living water of the

Gospel is like drawing water from a well. The content of the well will dictate the quality of the water drawn from it.

I have fond memories of spending time on my grandparents' farm in the hills of Tennessee. One special memory is two strategically located mountain springs that offered some of the cleanest, clearest and best tasting water in the world. Those springs illustrate a great truth for the preacher. We draw from the well of knowledge that we've gained throughout our years of life. We can only draw from the well what has been put into the well.

Both sets of my grandparents had underground wells from which they drew water to meet their needs. The water was always cool, clean and plentiful. The wells were fed, refreshed, filled and refilled by underground mountain springs flowing from higher ground.

They also had ponds of water used by the cattle and mules on the farm. My grandparents warned me not to drink water from the ponds. The water was not pure and clean. It contained bacteria and other harmful agents. The animals were used to the water but it would probably make me sick.

The water was stagnant because it sat idle with

no source of fresh water except from an occasional rain. Even then, much of the water drains into the ponds from the surrounding pasture that is filled with things that contaminate the water.

Preaching is much the same. When we stand before others to proclaim God's Word, we draw from our well of experiences and knowledge. Our preaching will become stagnant if we fail to add fresh, clean, cool springs to our well of knowledge and experiences.

Read, Read, and Read How can we add freshness to our preaching? My father is 87 years old and a great man. He provided for our family using his hands. He built cars for General Motors and could fix most anything that needed fixing around the house.

I'm the oldest son and was Dad's assistant on many of his homework projects. We worked together on cars, lawnmowers and a variety of other things.

Dad kept a toolbox filled with the basic tools necessary to do most jobs. I learned what a box end wrench, open end wrench, channel lock pliers, Phillips screwdriver, and a variety of other tools were. I also learned that the best and easiest way to do any job properly was to always use the correct tool.

One way of adding preaching tools to your

toolbox is by reading. Reading stretches the mind and expands the preacher's well of knowledge. Books to the preacher are like tools to the mechanic. The preacher uses the preaching tools he's accumulated in his preaching toolbox of knowledge to craft each sermon he prepares. The more tools he has accumulated, the more options he has building each part of his sermon.

The Bible, God's Holy Word, is the most important book and should take precedence over all other books. Even so, reading books written by men and women of good spiritual and intellectual reputation will add depth and power to your preaching. It will infuse clean, clear, and fresh material into your heart, mind, preaching and ministry.

Sit at Others' Feet – There are at least three ways you can do this.

First, listen to older preachers preach. You can gain a wealth of knowledge by observing older preachers, including reading their sermons. Be attentive to their style, their sermon introductions, use of words, intentional pauses, sermon structure, explanation and exegesis of Scripture. Notice how they draw the sermon together at its conclusion and how they compel others to make decisions at the close of the sermon.

Second, attend conferences, seminars, and workshops. You can expand your knowledge in specific areas by one to three days of intensive study. Learning from men and women with special expertise will increase and deepen your well of knowledge and place more tools in your preaching toolbox.

Third, enroll in courses and programs of study through a college, university, seminary, or Bible Institute. There are many opportunities for online study for pastors and preachers. Some courses are offered free or at a large discount. Ask for recommendations from other preachers. Investigate course offerings online. Pursue and complete a college degree if possible.

Final Thoughts

The key to successful preaching is purposeful preparation. This begins with preparing the heart through personal prayer, purity in lifestyle, and proficiency in the Scriptures.

It continues with expanding the well of knowledge and experience through preparing intellectually. This can be accomplished by becoming an avid reader. Reading will help you stay fresh mentally and breathe new life into your sermons.

Learn from others. Listen to older mature preachers preach. You can learn a great deal from them. Further your education by attending conferences, seminars, and workshops. Enroll in courses of study that will stretch your mind and expand your knowledge.

I close this chapter by reminding you of what I mentioned earlier from 2 Timothy 2:15: *Study so you will receive God's approval, a preacher who won't have to be ashamed of his sermons because he will be handling and proclaiming God's Word correctly* (my paraphrase).

Let's Begin

How does one take passages of Scripture and develop them into sermons? Below is a process that may be helpful.

We should always approach God's Word with awe and reverence. The first and most important thing we should do is pray, asking the Holy Spirit to help us see and understand the message of the passage.

Examine the Passage

1.   Always begin with the Bible.

2.   Read the entire passage.

3.   Carefully observe and seek to answer the basic questions of who, what, when, where, why, and how?

4.   *Who* is speaking? Who is being spoken to? Who are the main characters?

5.   *What* is the subject of the passage? What event or activity is being covered in the passage? What does the passage teach us about the people, event, or activity?

6. *When* does this passage take place? When did or will this event or activity mentioned take place?

7. *Where* did or will the activity or event mentioned take place? Where was this written or said?

8. *Why* is something being said or mentioned? Why did or will this happen? Why did or will this happen at this time? Why did or will this happen to this person or people? Why was this passage written?

9. *How* will this happen? How will it be done? How is it illustrated?

Interpret the Passage

Interpretation of the passage should follow the examination of the passage. Examination is scrutiny to understand what's being said. Interpretation is to understand the overall meaning of the passage.

Use what you have learned through examination to discern the primary meaning of the passage. You are seeking to discover what the biblical author was trying to communicate and also what God wants to communicate to you through the author and the passage.

Keep in mind: What biblical truth is God conveying in this passage? What prompted the author to write this passage? What sinful, broken, harmful, hurting, etc. condition is being addressed or corrected in the passage? What are the primary message and meaning of the passage? Which verses support the primary message?

I would encourage you to double check your thinking by looking at what others have written on the passage. Review commentaries, articles by conservative writers, Bible dictionaries, word meanings, etc.

Apply the Passage

Correct interpretation will lead to appropriate application of the passage. You should ask how this passage applies to you and others? What actions do you and others need to take in order to apply what God is communicating?

Summary

When you have examined the passage, interpreted and understand it, and determined how it should be applied, then you are ready to develop your sermon. The next two chapters will be a great help in learning the elements of sermons and how to develop the passage into a sermon.

Sound Biblical Homiletics

I remember walking into Mr. Ralph Hampton's Biblical Homiletics class the first semester of my junior year at Welch College. I had answered the call to preach in October of my freshman year before spending two years in the United States Armed Forces during the Vietnam War. I had completed my sophomore year, and now my college courses were focusing on my chosen profession as a minister.

I wasn't sure what to expect in Biblical Homiletics, but I began to realize the importance and value the course would have on my preaching.

The word homiletics comes from the Greek word ὁμιλητικός (homilitikos), from which we also get the word homily. The word literally means: *To assemble, to put many pieces together.* Sermons are, in a sense, biblical homilies constructed by putting various pieces together following recognized homiletics guidelines (my definition.)

William Goulooze has some great ideas on this subject. I want to give him credit for sparking my thinking and expanding on some of his ideas. Here are some great guidelines that may be helpful in putting pieces together that will become a sermon.

1. Use a text that has a spiritual truth at its core. The Bible is well constructed, offering many passages with emphasis on evangelism for the sinner and edification for the saint.

2. Read the text carefully, keeping in mind the context of the chapter and book of the Bible in which it appears. This is the key to learning and understanding the meaning of the passage.

3. Study the text, keeping in mind the meaning as written in its original language. There are resources available online that can help you with this.

4. Read the text in traditional and modern versions of the Bible. Looking at various translations with give you a wider perspective and help you focus on the meaning of the text.

5. Divide the text into divisions.

    a. Develop a simple, logical sentence that expresses the thought of the division.

    b. Develop a short rhetorical statement you can memorize and use when you preach the sermon later.

    c. Develop a quote from the text in

each division that forms the basis for the division.

      d. Develop your sub-divisions using the same process as the main divisions.

      6. Read commentaries and other sermons on the text. This will help you double check your theological, doctrinal, and exegetical conclusions to be sure you are on safe hermeneutical ground (correct method of interpretation).

      7. Decide on a theme for the entire passage. Develop a simple sentence summarizing the passage divisions.

      8. Determine and indicate the purpose of the message in its beginning, and also reflect it in the sermon's final form. Your purpose statement should reflect the theology, doctrine, exhortation, salvation, edification, and instruction found in the passage.

      9. Develop your invitation. A later chapter provides broader description and information regarding the development of invitations.

      10. Develop your conclusion. This may contain a story or example illustrating the purpose and theme of the message. Summarize the passage, making appropriate applications and challenging the hearers to make a commitment or decision. You'll find more detail and help writing your sermon conclusion

later in the book.

Final Thoughts

It is a given that prayer is one of the most important parts of sermon preparation. Quality study and in-depth thorough scholarship are vital to good sermon preparation.

Of equal importance is the Holy Spirit's guidance. You must do your part by providing the tools the Holy Spirit can use to impact your thinking and guide you as you prepare your sermons.

Putting the sermon pieces together in a prudent and effective way *(biblical homiletics)* is hard work. It requires time, talent and sometimes treasure, but it is worth it.

To impact the lives of others for a day or eternity is one of the greatest privileges one can have. We should do our best in preparing sermons, knowing that we have been given the privilege and that God is observing.

Using good biblical homiletics will help your sermons be the best they can be. You'll produce quality sermons with solid content that are easy for others to listen to and will have power that can change lives.

The Craft of Sermon Building

One fond memory I have of high school is a drafting course. My father took me to a special store in my hometown that sold architectural, engineering and blueprint design drawing instruments. He purchased a great set of precision drawing tools that I used in my drafting class.

I designed houses, a church, and other buildings. I learned the importance of step-by-step well thought out building design. I learned to look at and draw the buildings from three different vantage points: front, top, and side views. Each view was important and was crucial to a full understanding and accurate depiction of the building.

Sermon preparation is very similar. There are elements that should be present in each sermon. More will be discussed later on a step-by-step process on how to put the elements together.

What are necessary elements of a sermon?

Below is a list and description of these elements.

1.   ***The Introduction*** - The sermon introduction comes at the beginning of the message. It captures the attention of the audience and makes them want to hear more.

a.   *What is the purpose of the introduction?*   The purpose is to capture the audience's attention. How this is done is important. The sermon's text and message will dictate how the sermon should be introduced.

b.   *How long should the introduction be?* The length depends on a number of factors. The length will depend on how complicated the passage may be. Also, the first message on a series to be preached will need to be longer to introduce the series.

Generally, about five minutes for a 25-30 minute message should be adequate. Do not over load the wagon with a too-lengthy or complicated introduction. The time you lose at the beginning of the sermon cannot be made up at the end.

c.   *Make good use of your hearers' undivided attention.*   Each time the preacher stands before his hearers; he has their undivided attention. They listen attentively, not knowing what he might say or what new thing he may share with them. Their attention may be undivided, but it can be divided quickly and wander away from the sermon. You will have about two minutes at the beginning to capture their attention and lead them to want to hear more.

d. *Use a good illustration.* I often choose my introduction illustration after I complete writing my sermon. I think about it and pray over my choice.

e. *Transition to the Word of God.* You should transition from your illustration to God's Word. Move from the secular and personal to the spiritual and theological. Describe the passage, seeking to provide an overall understanding of the text to your hearers.

f. *Build a bridge from the introduction to the main body of the sermon.* This will guide your hearers to the main part of your sermon. This doesn't have to be lengthy, but it should clearly present the structure of your message and where you are heading.

The bridge will also guide your hearers through your message. A good bridge sentence includes a description of what is about to follow, such as: *We will look at (three, four or five) principles, steps, warnings, temptations, tests, etc.* This will be illustrated in more detail later.

2.   ***The Main Points*** – The main points are the skeleton upon which you place the meat of the sermon. Dividing the sermon into points has great value for the preacher and his listeners.

a.   *Dividing the sermon into points has value to the preacher.* Dividing the sermon into points or sections provides clear thinking for the preacher. The preacher's message must be clearly understood by his hearers.

Arranging his message in an organized manner helps the preacher clearly and distinctly convey his thoughts to his listeners. The message becomes clearer and lends itself to be remembered and presented even better by the preacher.

b.   *Dividing the sermon into points helps promote unity throughout the sermon.* Outlining material helps the flow and unity of the passage to be clearly understood by the preacher.

c. *Dividing the sermon into points helps the preacher better remember the message.* It is much easier for the preacher to remember the outline while he is preaching rather than constantly looking at his notes. He can keep better eye contact with the congregation and thus stay better connected with them.

d. *Here are some things to remember in developing the main points.*

- The main points should rise from the purpose of the sermon contained in the introduction with each main point helping define and develop it.

- Each main point should be distinct from the others.

- All the main points should have a logical, natural flow to them.

- The main points should develop, support, and defend the purpose of the sermon described in the introduction.

- Each main point should be limited to and contain one easily understood idea.

- The sermon should be limited to as few main points as possible. Too many main points will tend to drag the sermon out and lose the interest of hearers.

Some messages may require more main points. I have found the wise thing to do is divide the message into two parts and preach part 1 and part 2 in two separate messages.

- Use variety in developing your main points. Using the same words, principles, steps, etc., will cause your hearers to place their minds in neutral and wander away from you mentally while you are preaching.

- Main points should be structured the same. For instance, if a sentence is used in the first main point, sentences should be used in each of the following main points. One word, a phrase, etc. should follow the same pattern.

e. *Transitioning from one main point to the next is important.* Your listeners need a smooth transition from one main point to the next. If you are to keep their interest, using transition sentences to move from one point to another is crucial. Good transition sentences contain "trigger words" that signal to the hearer that a transition is about to be made.

Here is an example. Suppose the sermon purpose statement in the introduction said: *We're going to look at 3 important decisions Daniel made that forever changed his life*. After we've looked at the first important decision, a good transition sentence might be: *The second important decision Daniel made that forever changed his life was to.........* This statement lets your listener know that you are moving from the first main point to the second main point.

3. ***The Sub-Points*** - The sub-points follow and support the main points, providing detailed explanation of the main points.

a. *Sub-points are derived from the main points and should be developed in a logical manner from them.* Main points are like a subject with each sub point being a part of the subject. Each sub point must shed further light on the subject contained in the main point.

b. *Sub-points should be properly balanced, just as the main points are.* The pattern established in the first sub point should be carried throughout the section under the same main point.

c. *Sub-points should be limited to three or four at the most.*

d.   *Sub-points do not necessarily have to be listed in the order found in the text.* This is especially true with expository sermons.

4.   **The Conclusion** - I had the privilege of pastoring near the Atlantic Ocean in Savannah, Georgia. One of my church members taught me how to catch fresh shrimp using a casting net.

Everything had to be just right, and that was always accomplished by good preparation on his part. The best time to catch the shrimp was on the incoming tide. We used a midsized flat bottom metal boat and moved up into the shallow sloughs. We tried to surprise the shrimp that were trying to make it to the grasses where they would feed and hide until the tide began to recede again.

I learned to throw a cast net. The key was holding the net properly, tying off the net to my left wrist, holding the open part with my teeth and casting the net with a sweeping action with my right hand, letting it make a big circle, sinking in the open water. I would let the net almost sink to the bottom and then pull the rope that closed the net and captured the shrimp inside. Nothing tastes quite as good as fresh shrimp you have caught yourself.

The conclusion of the sermon is much like the principle of the cast net. It should be approached as the culmination of a process of preparation. Drawing the net is the ultimate goal of every sermon.

There are three elements that I usually include as part of the conclusion to my sermons.

a.   *Review* I review the main points of the sermon but generally do not recite them word for word.

b.   *Return to my introduction illustration*
I usually begin each message, after reading the text, with an illustration. I reach a point in the illustration where interest is high and people want to know the rest of the story. Then I pause…. and tell them I will share the rest of the story at the end of the message. I return to the illustration after reviewing the main points of the message and finish the story.

c.   *Relay the application of the text*
I apply the message of the text and transition into the invitation.

Here are some things to remember when writing your sermon conclusion.

•   Keep your conclusion brief. Be

careful about saying: *In conclusion or in closing* and then preaching another fifteen minutes. Respect your people and respect their expectations. If you announce you are about to conclude, then conclude!

• Keep your conclusion simple. Simple and plain language that is penetrating will be more effective than using elaborate words and language that tends to focus on the preacher more than the message he just preached.

• Carefully choose the final words of your conclusion. You should design your words to impress upon your audience the importance and urgency of the subject matter you've just preached.

5. **The Invitation** - Every message should include a challenge to the hearer and provide an opportunity to make a personal decision. The next chapter is dedicated to developing a good invitation.

6. **The Illustration -** Illustrations are used to help the audience understand the purpose and points found within the sermon. What is an illustration? I'm not sure where I read this but an illustration is to make clear by means of an example or examples. Illustrations are used like clear windows that bring

light to illuminate sermons. Please keep in mind that the most important part of every sermon is the Word of God, not illustrations. However, illustrations do have value and are important.

a. *Sermons become clearer with the use of illustrations.*

b. *Sermons are more interesting to listen to when illustrations are used.*

c. *Illustrations make truth stand out.*

d. *Here are some things to remember when selecting illustrations.*

• Use illustrations that are applicable to the point you are trying to make.

• Be sure the illustration can be clearly understood by your audience. You are wasting your time if they do not clearly understand the illustration.

• Use illustrations that have credibility. Believe me, with the Internet at everyone's fingertips; you will be fact-checked before the sun goes down. Failing to use credible illustrations will hurt your ministry. Your people may feel that you tend to exaggerate and that is never a good thing for a preacher.

• Tell the story correctly. Don't

embellish the story and twist it into a contorted shadow of the true story.

- Don't use long illustrations. Keep them brief. Otherwise, you may become too rushed with the rest of your sermon and leave out biblical truth that God wanted you to share.

- Use only illustrations that are in good taste. Crude, off-color or embarrassing illustrations should be left at the door and never brought to the pulpit.

- Keep good records of the illustrations you use. I made the mistake of repeating an illustration at a church I'd preached at years earlier. I learned my lesson.

7. **The Application** - Applying God's truth is one of the most important elements of the sermon. Applying God's Word enables individuals to focus on God's truth, what is expected of them, what changes they need to make, and how the truths brought out in the passage can impact their everyday lives.

a. *When should applications be made in sermons?*

- The time of the application depends on the content of the sermon.

• Normally, application should be made with each spiritual truth that is presented.

• Sometimes application is better made at the end of each sub-point or main point.

• Some sermons lend themselves to application being made at the conclusion of the sermon.

b. *Here are some things to remember when applying scripture.*

• Make the sermon relevant to the basic problems and needs that people face each day.

• Be creative in imagining and portraying Biblical characters in order to make them come alive in your preaching.

• Use illustrations that show how truth can be applied to people's everyday lives.

• Show truths from the text that are universal principles, applicable at all times.

• Do not add applications that are not visible in the passage.

• Make the applications specific and not general.

• Apply the truths with the right

motivation.

- Show that the truth you are applying is for our time here and now.

Giving the Invitation

Most of us understand what inviting someone over for dinner or joining us in an event means. The invitation element of the sermon encompasses much more. It means affording the opportunity to others to receive the wonderful blessings that come from the Gospel of Jesus Christ. It appeals for an internal decision expressed with an outward act.

The invitation is the critical part of every sermon. It is the destination towards which you have driven the whole sermon. It is the point where present and future meet for the hearer.

There is disagreement among preachers on whether invitations should be given during sermons. I believe invitations are biblical and should be part of the sermons we preach.

Roy Fish, in his book Giving a Good Invitation, gives some great reasons as to why we should give invitations during our sermons.

Why give invitations?

1. *The nature of the Gospel calls for an invitation.* When we look at the preaching by the apostles in the New Testament, it is obvious that their preaching and invitations were inseparable. The magnitude of the message demanded a response from the hearer.

The apostle Peter called for a response from his hearers after a compelling message at Pentecost in Acts 2:38. He gave an invitation to his hearers after his second message in Acts 3:19 where he said: *Repent therefore and turn back that your sins may be blotted out.* ESV

Jesus often compelled people to make decisions following his sermons. In Luke 13:3 Jesus said: *Unless you repent, you will also perish* (my paraphrase). He also said in Mark 1:15: *Repent and believe the Gospel.* ESV

The Gospel would be incomplete without an appeal to respond. The Gospel offers salvation and new life in Christ, but it presents this offer with an invitation to choose to receive it.

The Gospel message always requires an invitation.

2. *Man's nature calls for an invitation.* God

created mankind with the ability to think, feel and act. This first became obvious with Adam and Eve in the Garden of Eden mentioned in Genesis chapters two and three.

God made the fruit from all but one tree in the garden available to Adam and Eve. He only restricted the tree of the knowledge of good and evil. He created the first couple with the free will to make decisions. They made a bad choice and ate from the wrong tree. All of us are suffering because of their bad decision.

God made available to mankind the opportunity to choose him. He invites men and women to come to him. Mankind's nature requires an invitation.

3.   *Invitations are biblical.* There are several examples in the Bible that lend credibility to modern day sermon invitations.

Moses came down from Mount Sinai and the people were worshipping a golden calf. He gave an invitation to everyone present in Exodus 32:26 when he said: *Whoever is on the Lord's side, come to me* (my paraphrase). This a clear invitation to take a public stands for the Lord.

Joshua gathered all the tribes of Israel together challenged them to serve the Lord and abandon the gods of Egypt in Joshua 24:15: *Choose you this day whom you will serve; whether the gods your father served that were on the other side of the flood, or the gods of the Amorites in whose land you dwell: but for me and my house, we will serve the Lord. KJV*

Elijah presented a challenge from Mount Carmel in 1 Kings 18:21: *Make up your mind, if the Lord is God follow him, but if Baal is God then follow him* (my paraphrase).

The Bible is filled with examples of invitations for decisions after messages have been preached. The pattern is simple and obvious that men and women should be challenged to make decisions through our preaching.

How should invitations be given?

I usually step away from the pulpit, walk off the stage, and make my way down in front of my audience to deliver my invitation. I lay the groundwork for the closing invitation during the opening introduction of each message. I do this by beginning an illustration early in the introduction.

I try to elevate the interest and then announce that the rest of the story will be finished at the end of the message. I finish the story, using it as a powerful connection to invite people to make important personal spiritual decisions.

There are a number of things to remember that will help you deliver personal, powerful, and productive invitations. Roy Fish presents some great insights in his book <u>Giving a Good Invitation</u>. Below are ten quick things to remember when giving invitations.

1. *Give the invitation with a spiritually prepared mind.* We must remember that we are confronting people with decisions that may have eternal consequences. It is a matter of life and death and should be approached with that in mind. We have the help and hope that people need.

2. *Give the invitation confidently and with expectation.* We should give invitations with confidence that God wants something to happen. We should believe that people will respond and decisions will be made. We should believe that the message we preached came from the Lord and has power to change lives.

3. *Depend on the Holy Spirit while giving the invitation.* Remind yourself that only the Holy Spirit can convict sinners. Only the Holy Spirit can transform a life. While waiting to rise from my seat to preach, I pray and tell the Holy Spirit how much I believe in him

and ask him to help me. I realized early in ministry that he is the one who will convict and convince people.

4.   *Convey the invitation clearly.* Be specific in the invitation. People should understand exactly what they are being asked to do. Too broad an invitation can be confusing and lessen the value of decisions.

People may respond but be unsure of what they are responding to. I always ask people why they came forward. I want them to understand exactly what they are doing.

5.   *Handle the invitation honestly.* Follow through with what you say during invitations.

If you say; *we'll sing one more verse and if no one responds we'll close the invitation*, then close the invitation if no one comes forward. Do not say this will be the last verse and then say let's sing another and another.

If you need to extend the invitation, and you will from time to time, then apologize and say something like: *I know I said that would be the last verse. I hope you'll forgive me, but I feel impressed to extend the invitation for at least one more verse.* Your listeners can count and they remember what you say and will notice if you don't do what you said you would do.

6. *Be courteous while giving the invitation.* Give the invitation with a gentle spirit showing love, compassion, and patience. Never be unkind, embarrass, criticize, or bully an audience. You should show the gentleness of Christ, and your audience should hear the voice of Christ as you share the challenge during the invitation.

7. *Take enough time to give a thorough invitation.* Do not shortchange your invitations by spending too much time on other parts of your messages. Remember, the invitation is the critical point in the message.

Don't rush through it! You are making the appeal that could forever change peoples' lives. Do a thorough and complete job. You've wrapped the gift with the message; now finish it by tying it up with a beautiful bow of the invitation that completes the package.

8. *Give the invitation with authority.* We should not be ashamed or apologetic when giving invitations. We are offering people the greatest gift they could ever receive. We should speak with compassion but be firm and direct. People should know that this is a serious matter.

---

9.   *Give the invitation with sense of urgency.* During my first pastorate in Ahoskie, North Carolina, I gave one particular invitation that comes to mind. I'm not sure what I preached on that Sunday morning, but I remember one huge thing I said during the invitation.

The invitation had made its way through two or three verses, and I paused the invitation. I said something like: *I feel impressed to extend the invitation for one more verse. Someone may be here and this will be the last opportunity you have to accept Christ as Savior.*

There was a young lady in her twenties in attendance who heard the message. God was dealing with her, but she resisted and did not respond to the invitation. A few weeks later, I received a phone call in the middle of the night from her husband telling me that she had taken a gun and committed suicide after an argument.

Those words kept coming back to me: *Someone may be here and this will be the last opportunity you have to accept Christ.* It was her last opportunity.

We must give our invitations with sense that life and eternity are serious business. We must approach them with a sense of urgency and know that it could a matter of life and spiritual death.

10. *Give the invitation smoothly*. Transitioning into the invitation is important. Good communication before the message with those handling the invitation - musicians, worship leader, etc. - will help the invitation go more smoothly. Many preachers begin the invitation with prayer. Others ask the musician(s) to play softly. Others ask those in attendance to stand with heads bowed and eyes closed.

You should allow the Holy Spirit to guide you. Select the approach with which you feel most comfortable. You may want to try different approaches until you find the one that is most comfortable for you. Continue to develop and refine it. Work on your invitations until they almost become second nature and flow from you smoothly and naturally.

What are some different ways of giving invitations?

There are a variety of possible responses that may be sought during invitations. The responses may vary and the appropriate response should be sought for each invitation.

Here are a few different types of invitations that I use:

1. *Appeal for uplifted hands at the beginning of the invitation.*

Occasionally, I ask at the beginning of the invitation for folks to raise their hands to indicate a specific need in their lives and if they would like me to pray for them.

2. *Appeal to make decisions while standing.* I often ask people to bow their heads and close their eyes and challenge them to pray making specific commitments while standing at their seats.

3. *Appeal to raise hands indicating that a specific decision or commitment has been made.* I often ask people to raise their hands after I have prayed during the invitation to indicate that they have made a specific commitment or decision in their lives.

4. *Appeal to make a public commitment.* I often ask people to come forward if they would like to respond to a specific challenge that was given during the invitation.

5. *Appeal to talk to someone afterwards.* Some people are shy, embarrassed, or fear being singled out in public. I often encourage people to talk with others or me at the conclusion of the service.

What types of decisions should you seek?

1. *The decision to accept Christ as Savior.* The most important decision you can challenge people to make is to receive Christ as Savior. This appeal should be made in most invitations even if your major focus is on another matter.

2. *The decision to know and do God's will.*

3. *The decision to find peace.*

4. *The decision to find contentment and fulfillment.*

5. *The decision to belong and be accepted.*

6. *The decision to find true freedom.*

7. *The decision to have needs met.*

8. *The decision to be thankful.*

9. *The decision to make a special commitment.*

This is only a sampling of decisions that people can be challenged to make. There are many others that could have been included.

V.L. Stanfield in his book <u>Effective Evangelistic Preaching</u> shares a great list of contrasts of what Christ offers through salvation and a life lived for him. Below is a summary:

1. Fear – Christ offers Assurance.
2. Loneliness – Christ offers Fellowship.
3. Lack of meaning in life – Christ offers Purpose in living.
4. Inner conflict – Christ offers Peace.
5. Weakness – Christ offers Strength.
6. Uncertainty – Christ offers Certainty.
7. Change – Christ never Changes.
8. Guilt – Christ offers Forgiveness.
9. Hell – Christ offers Heaven.
10. Death – Christ offers Life.
11. Eternal separation – Christ offers Eternal Life.
12. Away from home – Christ offers a Home.
13. Cowardice – Christ offers Manliness.
14. Unfair play – Christ offers Fair Play.
15. Abnormality – Christ offers Normality.
16. Unreasonableness – Christ offers Reason.

Great care should be taken in giving invitations. Keep in mind the points mentioned in this chapter and they will provide a great resource to help you with your invitations.

My Sermon is Prepared, Now What?

Your sermon is finished and now it is time to preach it. How you handle yourself in the pulpit will have a positive or negative impact on the effectiveness of the sermon.

I remember preaching a weekend youth revival in a church when I was 18 years old. I had only preached three or four times in about five months since answering the call to preach. I was wearing a medium blue, double-breasted suit. I rose to speak and one of the buttons on my suit fell off, hit the top my shoe, rolled off the stage onto the hardwood floor, and came to rest beside the foot of the head deacon on the front row. I was so embarrassed, but I immediately launched into the message and said nothing about the button. I didn't want others to be distracted from the message.

We must remember that what we do from the stage and pulpit should be about Christ and not us. He is the one people need to hear and see. We should conduct ourselves in ways that will draw our hearers to the message and not away from it.

Common Sense Pulpit Principles

Here are some things to keep in mind.

Appearance

How we look while delivering God's Word is important. We must look our best. We should be alert to things that might detract from making our best impression.

1. Clothes – *Wear clothes that fit.* Clothes that are too tight or too loose will give a bad impression.

Wear clothes that are modest. Do not wear anything that will attract the wrong kind of attention.

Wear clothes that are clean, pressed, neat, and unwrinkled. Your clothes say something about you. They should look crisp and sharp. You will look crisp and sharp and represent the Lord well.

Make sure your shoes are clean and polished. Badly scuffed or dirty shoes tell those listening to you that you do not pay attention to the little things.

Wear a belt. Empty belt loops often convey a

sloppy look to your people and they may equate it with laziness.

Wear clothes that will help your people rise to the next level. Dressing down seems to be a hit with many preachers today. Ragged jeans, tee shirts, sandals, no socks, and even being barefoot have become standard dress for some.

I am sure that I am old school, but I firmly believe that we should not try to dress down to become more like the world around us, but dress at least one level above to help elevate our people to a higher plain.

How would you dress if you were going to see the governor of your state? You see the God of your universe every time you step into the pulpit.

IBM, a great United States Company, had an expression, *Dress for Success*. They believed this so greatly that they insisted their employees dress in a way that conveyed a message to the public that they are professionals.

The profession of preacher requires him to dress for success. This does not necessarily mean a coat and tie. It does mean he should be neat, clean, modest, and one step above his hearers.

2.   Personal Hygiene – We should prepare our

bodies to stand in front of others to preach God's Word.

Take a shower or bath and make sure you are clean when you stand to preach. The Old Testament is filled with passages that required priests to wash themselves and their clothes and to enter the tent of meeting or temple clean.

Brush your teeth and make sure your breath is not offensive.

Comb your hair and make sure your hair, beard and mustache are clean and neatly trimmed. Unkempt, oily hair that needs cutting sends a signal of unprofessionalism to your people. Your hair should look fresh, clean and neat.

Keep your fingernails clean and trimmed. People will notice if you have dirt under your nails or if they are ragged looking and need trimming. It conveys a message that your hands may be dirty. The attention of your hearers may become focused on your hands rather than your message.

Eye Contact

Eye contact with your audience is important. You must connect with your hearers on multiple levels. One of these levels is with your eyes.

1. *Each person in the room should feel that you are speaking directly to him or her.* One of the best ways to do this is with eye contact. I do my best to make eye contact with as many people one-on-one as I can during the message.

2. *Be careful not to focus too much on one person or one side of the room.* You need to be deliberate with this.

3. *Double-check yourself when you are speaking.* Ask: *Am I looking at this person too much? Am I looking only to my right or my left and leaving the other side of the room out? Am I moving only to one side of the stage?*

Something that has helped me is to move from one side of the stage to the other during the message. I have found that this helps people feel that I am speaking to them when I move to their side of the stage. I repeat and alternate this at appropriate times throughout the message.

4. *Be careful not to look over the heads of your congregation.* It will be distracting if you choose to look at something in the back of the room. Your people will feel that you are looking beyond them and not feel as connected. I have seen many preachers do this and observed their congregations looking away

from the stage. They begin to daydream and think of things other than the message.

Gestures

Gestures can add to the interest and impact of the sermon. They can also distract and detract from the sermon.

1.   *Be conscious of what you are doing with your hands.* Never put your hands in your pocket while preaching. Be careful about repetitive actions with your hands. Doing the same thing over and over again will cause your hearers to focus on your hands and not on your message.   Use both hands, alternating them when gesturing. Your hearers will notice you are using only one hand.

2.   *Facial gestures can add to the power of sermons and should be expressive.* A smile at the appropriate time can bring smiles to the faces of your hearers. A sympathetic look can pull the emotions of sympathy form the audience. A sad look can help the audience feel sad for the person or biblical character. A glance off into the distance can help the audience see something in their mind's eye over the horizon or in the direction you are looking.

3.   *Body language can communicate a great deal.*

You can literally paint a picture for your audience as you stand, slouch, throw out your chest, raise your arms, wave, throw your head back, drop to one knee, slap the podium, turn and face another direction, stand tall, look confident, look weak, limp, wink, sit down, walk fast across the stage and a variety of other things.

Train yourself to recognize opportunities to use body language during each message. Soon it will become natural and your confidence level will continue to grow.

Voice

Your voice is a great tool God has given you to preach his Word. You may be thinking; *of course I will need my voice to preach. What is he talking about?*

Here are some things to keep in mind about using your voice when delivering your sermons.

1.   *Speak loud enough to be heard.* Do not speak so softly that people have trouble hearing you. With the good sound systems that most of our churches possess today, this is normally not a problem.

2.   *Do not yell and scream so loud that people cannot understand what you are saying.*   I like emotion in preaching. I believe it adds to the sincerity of sermons. But if you scream or yell so loud that it hurts peoples' ears or your speech is not understandable because of it, you will turn people off and they will not receive what you are offering.

3.   *Do not speak in a false heavenly voice that appears to be more spiritual than those listening to you.* I have heard preachers deepen their voices to sound more spiritual.

4.   *Try not to speak in a monotone.* Change your voice inflection from softer to louder, lower to higher, higher to lower, etc.

5.   *Try not to speak too fast.* Speak fast enough to keep your message moving but slow enough to allow each part of your sermon to be heard and understood.

6.   *Learn to pause at different points during your message.* Calculated pauses have been used effectively as long as speakers have been speaking to audiences. I love to stop and pause after a powerful point or statement has been made. My audiences sometimes seem to be on the edge of their seats waiting to hear the next statement or the end of some

story.

7. *Keep a bottle or cup of water handy.* I try to always have a bottle of water with me when I stand to preach. Wordcounter.net estimates that the average preacher uses approximately 1000 – 2000 words per minute during his message. Multiply that by 30 minutes and you'll be speaking about 30,000 to 60,000 words per message. Your mouth and throat can become very dry. Words become hard to pronounce and your mouth feels like you have cotton in it. The water helps greatly.

Final Thoughts

God created you and then called you to preach. Do not try to preach like someone else. Learn from others, but be who you are! Become the best preacher you can be. You should always be looking for ways to improve and become a better preacher.

Work on your weaknesses and build on your strengths. Ask for constructive criticism and accept it humbly.

Pray and ask the Lord to help you preach with boldness and effectiveness. Recognize that without him and the help of his Holy Spirit your messages will be weak and the impact on the lives of others will be minimal.

Your sermon is prepared. Now what? Preach... Preach... Preach.

Helpful Ideas and Themes

Here are some simple, creative, and easy-to-remember sermon ideas that may be helpful.

This article is from Pastors.com

Adrian Rogers outlined sermons using four phrases:

Hey You! (Get the audience's attention)

Look! (Examine the Scriptures)

See! (Explain the passage)

Do! (Make application)

Andy Stanley is famous for one-point preaching, but really breaks his messages into five movements:

Me (How do I struggle with this?)

We (How do we all struggle with this?)

God (What does the Bible say about this?)

You (What should you do about this?)

We (How can we all live this out together?)

Another *well-known system* is:

Hook (Get attention)

Book (Examine the Word)

- Look (Expound the passage)

Took (Make an appeal)

Top 50 Sermon Themes of All Time

(Share Faith Magazine - https://www.sharefaith.com)

1. **Sermons on the Love of God**

   John 3:16, 1 John 4:7-12, 1 John 5:1-5, Romans 8:38-39, Romans 5:8, 2 Chronicles 9:8, Deuteronomy 7:9

2. **Sermons on the Greatness of God**

   Genesis 1, 1 Peter 1:20, Romans 8:38-39, Romans 1:20, John 17:5, John 17:24, Isaiah 55:9, Isaiah 40:28, Psalm 90:2, Psalm 19:1

3. **Sermons on Peace**

   Psalm 46:10, Psalm 122:6-7, John 14:27, Philippians 4:8, 2 Thessalonians 3:16, John 16:33, Romans 12:18, Hebrews 12:14, Proverbs 16:7, Galatians 5:22, Romans 14:19

4. **Sermons on the Strength of God**

   Psalm 27:1, Psalm 73:26, Psalm 16:8, Nahum 1:7, Isaiah 41:10, Philippians 4:13, Isaiah 40:29, Psalm 119:28

5. **Sermons on Prayer**

   Philippians 4:6-7, Matthew 26:36-46, 1 John 5:14, Matthew 6:9-13, Matthew 7:7, 1 Thessalonians 5:16-18, Luke 11:1-4, 2 Chronicles 7:14

6. **Sermons on Creation**

   Jeremiah 51:15, Genesis 1:1, Isaiah 64:8, Luke 1:37, Psalm 8:3, 1 Corinthians 8:6,

7. **Sermons on Hope**

   1 Timothy 4:10, Psalm 147:11, Jeremiah 29:11, Romans 15:13

8. **Sermons on the Crucifixion of Christ**

   John 20:25, Romans 8:39, John 19:30, John 15:13, Romans 10:9, Romans 5:8, 1 Peter 2:24, Luke 23:46

9. **Sermons on Satan**

   Revelation 12:9-10, Ephesians 6:11-12, 1 Peter 5:8, 1 John 3:8, 2 Corinthians 11:3, 2 Corinthians 11:14, John 10:10

10. **Sermons on Marriage**

    Ephesians 5:22-28, Mark 10:7-9, 1 Corinthians 13:4-7, Ecclesiastes 4:12, Hebrews 13:4, Genesis 2:24, 1 Peter 3:1-5

11. **Sermons on the Sovereignty of God**

    Psalm 91:9-10, Job 38, Colossians 1:16, 1 Chronicles 29:11, Isaiah 45:7, Psalm 147:4-5

12. **Sermons on the Resurrection**

Romans 8:39, Matthew 26:36-36, Matthew 28:6, 1 Peter 1:3, 1 Corinthians 15:55

13. **Sermons on the Holy Spirit**

John 8:36, Acts 2:3-4, Titus 3:5b-6, John 3:6-8, Ephesians 5:18, 2 Timothy 1:7

14. **Sermons on Spiritual Warfare**

Matthew 5:30, Ephesians 6:12, Ephesians 6:16, Hebrews 4:12

15. **Sermons on Being a Godly Father**

Genesis 1:26-5:5 (Adam), Genesis 5-10 (Noah), Genesis 11-25 (Abraham), Genesis 17, 21-22, 24-28, 31, 35 (Isaac), Genesis 25-37, 42, 45-49 (Jacob), Exodus (Moses), 1 Samuel 16 – 1 Kings 2 (King David), Matthew 1:16-2:23 (Joseph)

16. **Sermons on Being a Godly Mother**

Genesis 1-4 (Eve), Genesis 12-23 (Sarah), Genesis 26-27 (Rebekah), Genesis 29-35 (Rachel), Exodus 1-2 (Jochebed), Ruth 1-4 (Naomi), 1 Samuel 1-2 (Hannah), Luke 1-2 (Mary)

17. **Sermons on Women of the Bible**

Esther 1-8 (Esther), 1 Samuel 1 (Hannah), Joshua 2:8-15 (Rahab),

18. **Sermons on Love**

1 Corinthians 13:4-8, John 15:13, Matthew 22:37-

39, 1 John 3:1, Mark 10:7-8

19. **Sermons on New Beginnings**

2 Corinthians 5:17, Acts 3:19-21, Ezekiel 36:24-28, Revelation 21:1-8, Isaiah 43:1-28

20. **Sermons on New Birth**

John 3:1-7, 2 Corinthians 5:17, Romans 6:1-11, Galatians 5:19-26

21. **Sermons on Great Bible Characters**

Exodus 3:10-22 (Moses), Genesis 37 (Joseph), 1 Samuel 17 (David), Book of Daniel (Daniel), Genesis 17 (Abraham)

22. **Sermons on the Christmas Story and Incarnation**

1 John 3:1, John 1:4, Matthew 2, Luke 1: 26-38, Luke 2:1-21

23. **Sermons on Thankfulness and Thanksgiving**

1 Thessalonians 5:16-18, Matthew 6:25-34, Ephesians 3:20-21, Philippians 4:4-7

24. **Sermons on Direction in Life**

Hosea 14:9, Proverbs 3:5-6, Proverbs 16:9, Psalm 37:23-24, Psalm 23:3, John 14:6

25. **Sermons on Faith**

Matthew 18:3, Hebrews 11, Mark 11:22-24, James 2:14-26, 2 Corinthians 5:7

26. **Sermons on God's Word, the Bible**

2 Timothy 3:16, Hebrews 4:12, Proverbs 4:20-22, Colossians 3:16, John 1:1, Psalm 119:105

27. **Sermons on Worship**

Psalm 29:2, Romans 12:1, Colossians 3:14-17, Isaiah 12, Psalm 96

28. **Sermons on Seeking God**

Luke 11:9, Matthew 7:7-11, Deuteronomy 4:29, Proverbs 8:17, Jeremiah 29:12-14, Matthew 6:33, Proverbs 2:4

29. **Sermons on Abundant Life**

John 10:10, Jeremiah 29:11, Ephesians 3:20-21, Psalm 1:1-3

30. **Sermons on Christian Community**

Matthew 26:35-37, 1 John 1:7, Hebrews 10:24-25, Acts 2:42-47

31. **Sermons on Christian Unity**

Philippians 2:2, 1 Corinthians 1:10, Romans 15:6, Ephesians 4:1-6, Romans 12:4-5

32. **Sermons on Trinity**

Matthew 28:19, John 14:26, Romans 8:9-11

33. **Sermons on Facing Giants**

Psalm 18:2, Ephesians 6:12, 1 Samuel 17, James 4:7, 2 Corinthians 10:4-5

34. **Sermons on Spiritual Growth**

Hebrews 5:12, Colossians 1:9-10, 1 Peter 2:1-25,
2 Peter 3:18

35. **Sermons on God's Provision**

Matthew 6:27-28, Philippians 4:4-7, Exodus 16:4,
2 Corinthians 9:8-11, Jeremiah 29:11

36. **Sermons on Finding Your Calling**

Ephesians 4:1-7, Luke 14:25-33, Hebrews 12:1-2,
2 Timothy 2:1-7

37. **Sermons on Grace**

1 Peter 5:10, Hebrews 4:16, Titus 3:4-7, Romans
6:14, Romans 5:8, John 4:1-45

38. **Sermons on Your Speech**

Proverbs 18:21, Matthew 12:36-37, Luke 6:45,
Psalm 19:14, Ephesians 4:29

39. **Sermons on the Joy of the Lord**

Romans 15:13, Nehemiah 8:10, Psalm 16:11,
Luke 15:10

40. **Sermons on Missions**

Matthew 28:19, Mark 16:15, Romans 1:16

41. **Sermons on Believing**

James 1:6, Matthew 17:20, Hebrews 11:1, John
20:6-9

42. **Sermons on Wisdom**

James 3:17, Book of Proverbs, Daniel 2:21, Psalm
111:10

43. **Sermons on Forgiveness**

Psalm 103:12, Matthew 6:14-15, Ephesians 1:7, Isaiah 1:18

44. **Sermons on Hope in Christ**

Psalm 147:11, Jeremiah 29:11, 1 Corinthians 15:54-55, Romans 15:13, Luke 2:11

45. **Sermons on Abiding**

John 15:5, John 14:6, John 8:31, 1 John 2:6, Psalm 91:1-16

46. **Sermons on the Church**

1 John 1:7, Colossians 1:18, Acts 2:42-47, Matthew 16:18, 1 Corinthians 3:11, Ephesians 2:19-22,

47. **Sermons on Tithes and Offerings**

Malachi 3:9-10, 2 Corinthians 9:7, Luke 6:38, Matthew 6:1-4, Mark 12:41-44

48. **Sermons on Baptism**

Matthew 3:17, Acts 2:36-38, John 3:5, Romans 6:3-4, Ephesians 4:4-6

49. **Sermons on Communion**

Matthew 26:26-28, 1 Corinthians 11:25, John 6:53-58, Luke 22:19-20

50. **Sermons on Lent**

Matthew 6:16-18, Joel 2:12-13, Matthew 4:1-11, 1 Peter 5:6-7

Preaching Series of Sermons

William Goulooze published an excellent book in 1956 titled <u>Success in Series Preaching</u>. The book includes about 1500 series preaching suggestions. It was reprinted as a mass-market addition in 1982. I would encourage you to pick up a copy of this book.

Developing and preaching series of sermons can be very rewarding and beneficial to the preacher. Series preaching helps the preacher know what he will be preaching for weeks at a time. It helps him plan his preaching schedule and also builds a long-term plan of preaching. It offers him an organized approach to sermon planning and preaching.

Preaching sermon series is also beneficial to the congregation. It helps them focus on a particular book of the Bible, words connected in Scripture, Bible characters, doctrinal truths, theological revelations, the life of Christ, and a variety of other things.

The congregation can become more knowledgeable of the Bible and mature in their

Christian lives. The congregation has a sense of direction in knowing what subjects the preaching will be covering.

Remember that successful series preaching requires each sermon to stand on its own, yet remain related to the whole series. You may wonder how you can come up with ideas for sermon series and how to develop them. Here are some suggestions.

1. Look for ideas for a series.

2. Pay close attention to what others are preaching. Many times you can get ideas from what others are doing.

3. Pay close attention to your congregation. Notice what they are concerned about or what currently interests them.

4. Be knowledgeable about current events. Preaching can include events happening around your people, in their neighborhoods, in your state, in the nation, and in the world.

5. Write down ideas. Keep notes on your phone. Keep a file on your laptop or desktop computer. List possible series subject ideas.

6. Be alert as you read Scripture to possible sermon topics and how the Scripture lends itself to messages that could well become a series.

7.   Keep the series topic in the back of your mind. Jot down sermon ideas, main points, and sub-points as you think of them and let them sleep, coming back to them time and time again.

8.   As you develop your preaching plan for the year, incorporate your sermon series into the preaching schedule.

9.   Announce the series to your congregation including the topic, subjects you'll cover, approximate number of sermons in the series, and the time frame in which you plan to preach them.

10.   Stick to what you told your congregation. Do not stop in the middle of the series. Doing what you said will earn credibility with your people.

11.   The length of series will be different from one preacher to the other. Most of my sermon series were limited to a maximum of about a dozen. Occasionally the topic required more, and I did not hesitate to preach more. At other times, I preached less. Be careful not to make the series last too long. Your congregation may become tired, bored and weary.

Sermon Series Ideas

Below are several ideas that may be developed into full-blown series of sermons. I've gleaned ideas for many of these sermon series below from several men through the years – Adrian Rogers, Allen Carr, Joel Gregory, Ed Hargis, David Jeremiah and several others. Please feel free to use, change, add to, or take away from what you find below. These are sermon title ideas designed to spark your thinking as you develop sermons and preach the Word.

A Study of the Judges of Israel

01 - Othniel: The Lion Of God - Judges 2:20-3:11

02 – Lefty Did It - Judges 3:12-30

03 - Shamgar: The Obscure Savior - Judges 3:31

04 - Deborah: A Woman Of Conviction And Courage - Judges 4:1-24

05 - The High Cost Of Low Living - Judges 6:1-10

06 - The Call Of Gideon - Judges 6:11-24

07 - The Cultivation Of Gideon - Judges 6:25-32

Home Improvement

01 - One Plus One Equals One - Mathew 19:4-6

02 - A Firm Family Foundation - Genesis 2:18-25

03 - Let's Talk - Ephesians 4:25-5:2

04 - The Case For Godly Manhood –
Ephesians 5:21-6:4

05 - The Case for Godly Womanhood- 1 Timothy 2:9-15

06 - Parenting By The Book - Deuteronomy 6:1-9

07 - Growing Up Together - Ephesians 6:1-4

Biblical Worship:
What It Is And Why It Matters

01 - The Synopsis Of Biblical Worship - John 4:20-30

02 - The Setting Of Biblical Worship - Genesis 22:1-18

03 - The Sacrifice Of Biblical Worship, Part 1 -
Deuteronomy 26:1-11

04 - The Sacrifice Of Biblical Worship, Part 2 -

Matthew 2:1-12

05 - The Scent Of Biblical Worship - Exodus 30:34-38

06 - The Significance Of Biblical Worship - Exodus 33:12-23

Joseph: God Meant It For Good

The Baptist Deacon Series

Jesus: The Suffering Servant

Back To The Future

(Expository Sermons On the Book of Revelation)

01 - The Unveiling Of The Book - Revelation 1:1-3

02 - A Sneak Preview Of Coming Attractions - Revelation 1:4-8

03 - I, John - Revelation 1:9-11; 18

04 - The Lord Of Glory - Revelation 1:12-18; 20

05 - The Lord of Glory In His Ministry - Revelation 1:12-19

06 - When The Flame Becomes An Ember - Revelation 2:1-7

07 - The Rich Little Poor Church - Revelation 2:8-11

08 - The Church That Married The World - Revelation 2:12-17

09 - The Church That Compromised With The World - Revelation 2:18-29

10 - An Autopsy Of A Dead Church - Revelation 3:1-6

11 - The Church Of The Open Door - Revelation 3:7-13

12 - Laodicea: You Make Me Sick - Revelation 3:14-22

13 - Going to Be Moving - Revelation 4:1

14 - Inside The Throne Room Of God - Revelation 4:2-11

15 - Worthy Is The Lamb - Revelation 5:1-7

Great Invitations Of The Bible
(Expository Sermons on the Great Invitations in the Bible.)

The Invitation To Commitment - Genesis 7:1-16

The Invitation To Companionship - Numbers 10:29-32

The Invitation To Cleansing - Isaiah 1:18

The Invitation To Contentment - Isaiah 55:1-3

The Invitation To Contrition - Hosea 6:1-2

The Invitation To Children - Matthew 19:13-15

The Invitation To Consider - John 1:35-42

The Invitation Of Confidence - John 6:37-40

The Invitation Of Conversion - Revelation 22:17

The Invitation Of Completion - Revelation 22:20

The Prison Experiences Of The Bible

The Prison Of His Promotions -
Genesis 39:20-22; 41:14

The Prison Of His Purifications - Judges 16:16-30

The Prison Of His Persuasions - Matthew 11:1-11

The Prison Of His Perseverance - Jonah 1:1-17

The Prison Of His Power - Acts 12:1-19

The Prison Of His Purposes - Jeremiah 32:1-15

The Prison Of His Praises - Acts 16:16-26

David: A Man After God's Own Heart
(24 Expository Sermons on the Life of King David)

How God Chooses - 1 Samuel 16:1-13

How God Builds A King - 1 Samuel 16:14-23

Surviving Giant Country - 1 Samuel 17:32-40

In The Presence Of True Greatness -
1 Samuel 18:5-16

The Prince And The Pauper - 1 Samuel 18:1-4

Learning To Lean - 1 Samuel 21:10-15

Climbing Out Of Your Cave - 1 Samuel 22:1-4

Responding Properly To Your Enemies -
1 Samuel 24:1-22

Analyzing An Angry Man - 1 Samuel 25:2-44

When Smart People Make Foolish Decisions -
1 Samuel 27:1-12

How Are The Mighty Fallen - 1 Samuel 31:1-13

The Bible: God's Perfect Word

Behold The Lamb

Behold The Lamb Promised - Genesis 3:1-21

Behold The Lamb Prepared - Luke 1:26-38

Behold The Lamb Provided - Luke 2:1-20

Behold The Lamb Praised - Luke 2:21-38

Behold The Lamb Presented - Hebrews 10:10-14

Lord, Teach Us To Pray

Prayer Is About Resting - Matthew 6:9

Prayer Is About Reverencing - Matthew 6:9

Prayer Is About Reigning - Matthew 6:10

Prayer Is About Resigning - Matthew 6:10

Prayer Is About Requesting - Matthew 6:11

Prayer Is About Releasing - Matthew 6:12

Prayer Is About Relying - Matthew 6:13

Prayer Is About Rejoicing - Matthew 6:13

Moments With The Master

A Transforming Moment - Mark 1:40-45

A Tragic Moment - Mark 10:17-22

A Terrifying Moment - John 8:1-11

A Touching Moment - Mark 5:22-34

A Tearful Moment - Mark 5:21-43

A Teaching Moment - John 3:1-15

A Thrilling Moment - Luke 23:32-43

A Tender Moment - John 21:1-19

A Trusting Moment - John 4:1-30

God's Lost And Found Department

The Lost Sheep - Luke 15:1-7

The Lost Silver - Luke 15:8-10

The Lost Son - Luke 15:11-24

The Lost Sibling - Luke 15:25-32

Abraham: Following in the Footsteps of Faith

The Call To A Life Of Faith - Genesis 11:27-12:3

Abram's Commitment To A Life Of Faith -
Genesis 12:4-9

The Truth About The Path To Egypt -

The Decalogue: The Ten Commandments

The Ten Commandments, An Introduction -
Exodus 20:1-17

Who Is On First - Exodus 20:1-3

No Pictures Allowed - Exodus 20:4-6

God's Last Name Is Not a Curse Word - Exodus 20:7

Sunday Is Still A Holy Day - Exodus 20:8-11

Honor Thy Father And Thy Mother - Exodus 20:12

There Is More To Murder Than Taking A Life -
Exodus 20:13

The Destructive Power Of Adultery - Exodus 20:14

Thou Shalt Not Steal - Exodus 20:15

How To Handle Your Neighbor's Reputation -
Exodus 20:16

The Sin Nobody Will Admit - Exodus 20:17

Joshua: Claiming Your Canaan

This Land Is Our Land - Joshua 1:1-18

She's Not The Girl She Used To Be - Joshua 2:1-24

How To Get Past Your Jordan - Joshua 3:1 - 4:24

Are You Ready To Claim Your Canaan? -
Joshua 5:1-13

The Book of Ruth: Pursued by Grace

Redeemed, Redeemed By Love Divine - Ruth 3:9-4:12

Somebody Pinch Me, Please - Ruth 4:13-22

Elijah, The Prophet of Confrontation and Courage

A Man Sent From God - 1 Kings 17:1

Dry Brook University - 1 Kings 17:2-7

Empty Barrel Graduate School - 1 Kings 17:8-16

Elijah's On The Job Training - 1 Kings 17:17-24

The Hireling And The Servant - 1 Kings 18:1-16

It's Show Time - 1 Kings 18:16-40

A Prophet's Work Is Never Done - 1 Kings 18:40-46

How The Mighty Are Fallen - 1 Kings 19:1-4

How The Fallen Are Restored - 1 Kings 19:1-21

Back In The Saddle Again - 1 Kings 19:15-51

When God says, "That's Enough!" - 1 Kings 21:17-29

Waiting On The Whirlwind - 2 Kings 2:1-14

Portraits of Jesus in John's Gallery

Jesus: The Word Of God - John 1:1-18

Jesus: The Son Of Man - John 2:1-11

Jesus: The Divine Teacher - John 3:1-21

Jesus: The Soul Winner - John 4:1-30

Jesus: The Great Physician - John 5:1-9

Jesus: The Bread Of Life - John 6:22-35

Jesus: The Fountain Of Living Water - John 7:37-39

Jesus: The Sympathetic Savior - John 8:1-11

Jesus: The Light Of The World - John 9:1-11

Jesus: The Good Shepherd - John 10:1-16

Jesus: The Resurrection And The Life - John 11:18-27

Jesus: The King - John 12:12-19

Jesus: The Humble Servant - John 13:1-20

Jesus: The Great Encourager - John 14:1-31

Jesus: The True Vine - John 15:1-11

Jesus: The Great Gift-Giver - John 16:7-15

Jesus: The Great High Priest - John 17:1-26

Jesus: The Model Sufferer - John 18:1-14

Jesus: The Crucified King - John 19:1-18

Jesus: The Resurrected Redeemer - John 20:1-18

Jesus: The Friend Of The Fallen - John 21:1-19

The Book of Romans

The Credentials Of Paul The Apostle Part 1 - Romans 1:1

The Credentials Of Paul The Apostle Part 2 -

The Book of Revelation

The Fall Of Religious Babylon - Revelation 17:1 - 18

The Fall Of Commercial Babylon - Revelation 18:1-24

Scenes Of Glory In Heaven - Revelation 19:1-10

VE Day - Revelation 19:11-21

The 1,000 Year Party - Revelation 20:1-10

The Sinner's Day In God's Courthouse -
Revelation 20:11-15

A Bright New World - Revelation 21:1-8

A Glimpse Of Our New Home - Revelation 21:9 - 22:5

The Conclusion Of The Book - Revelation 22:6-21

(To give credit where credit is due, this series draws heavily upon the work of Dr. Jerry Vines. This sermon series was prepared back in the late 1980's. Dr. Vines preached this series while he was Pastor at West Rome Baptist Church in Rome, GA in the early 1970's. His skill, research and work in the biblical text formed much of the basis for this series. Thank you, Dr. Vines.)

A Biblical View of the End Times

When Trumpets Fade - 1 Corinthians 15:51-58; 1 Thessalonians 4:13-18

The Truth About Satan's Superman - Daniel 8:23-27

The Time Of Jacob's Trouble - Matthew 24:1-31

Heaven's Coronation Day - 1 Corinthians 3:10-15

A Marriage Made In Heaven - Revelation 19:1-9

The King Is Coming - Revelation 19:11-21

1,000 Years Of Heaven On Earth - Revelation 20:1-10

Nowhere To Hide - Revelation 20:11-15

A Glimpse Of A Place Called Hell - Luke 16:19-31

A Glimpse Of A Place Called Heaven -
Revelation 21:1-27

Basic Bible Doctrines

How To Be Saved And Know It - 1 John 5:11-13

How To Come Back When You Are Down -
Psalm 51:1-19

God's Formula For Fellowship - 1 John 1:1-10

How To Tame Temptation - 1 Corinthians 10:12-14

How To Have A Spirit-Filled Life - Ephesians 5:18

The Chemistry Of The Cross - Romans 8:28

The Road Map To Maturity - 1 Corinthians 2:14-3:1

How To Know The Will Of God - Acts 9:1-6

How To Practice The Presence Of God - Acts 7:47-49

Powerful Principals For Proper Practice -

1 Corinthians 6:12

(Please note: This series of sermons was first preached by Dr. Adrian Rogers, when he was the Pastor of Bellevue Baptist Church in Memphis, TN. Dr. Rogers' outlines can be found at this link: http://www.bellevue.org/).

Can God?

Can God? - Psalm 78:12-20

Can God Really Save Your Soul? - John 3:16-17

Can God Really Meet Your Need? - 1 Kings 17:1-24

Can God Really Save Your Loved Ones? - Luke 16:19-31

Can God Really Use Your Life? - Acts 9:1-16

Home and Family Series

A Marriage Made In Paradise - Genesis 2:18-25 (Marriage)

The World's Greatest Undertaking - Deuteronomy 6:1-9 (Child Raising)

From Dreadlock To Wedlock - Ephesians 5:22-33
(Marriage)

God's Word To Married Couples - 1 Corinthians 7:1-5
(Marriage)

God's Word To Singles - 1 Corinthians 7:6-9
(Single Life)

God's Word To The Separated - 1 Corinthians 7:10-16
(Marriage, Divorce and Remarriage)

God's Word About Your Money - Mark 12:41-44
(Finances and Giving)

Prayer Series

The Place Of Prayer - Luke 18:1

The Privilege Of Prayer - Psalm 55:16-17

The Pattern For Prayer - Matthew 6:9-13

The Problems Of Prayer - Psalm 66:18

Bibliography

The following were great resources I read and used in writing this book.

Braga, James *How to Prepare Bible Messages*, 1981, Multnomah Press, Portland, Organ.

Carr, Alan *The Sermon Notebook*, https://www.sermonnotebook.org/index.htm

De Brand, Roy E. *Guide to Biographical Preaching*, 1988, Broadman Press, Nashville, Tennessee.

Fasol, Al A *Guide To Self-Improvement in Sermon Delivery*, 1983, Baker Book House, Grand Rapids, Michigan.

Fish, Roy L. *Giving a Good Invitation*, 1974, Broadman Press, Nashville, Tennessee.

Goulooze, William *Success in Series Preaching*, 1982, Baker Book House, Grand Rapids, Michigan.

Hostetler, Michael J. *Introducing The Sermon*, 1986, Zondervan Publishing House, Grand Rapids, Michigan.

Preachers Worth Hearing

The following is a list of some my favorite preachers. Not all have works in print, but you might enjoy researching these, listening to them on YouTube, and reading their materials where possible.

Dr. W.A. Criswell

Dr. Billy Graham

Dr. Joel Gregory

Reverend Ed Hargis

Reverend Aaron Harris (my son)

Reverend Van Dale Hudson

Dr. Jack Van Impe

Dr. David Jeremiah

Reverend Bobby Jackson

Dr. B.R. Lakin

Reverend Jack Paramore

Reverend Larry Powell

Dr. Adrian Rogers

Dr. Charles Thigpen

Reverend Jonathon Thigpen

Dr. Jerry Vines

Dr. Jack Williams

Sermons From My Notes

The following pages contain a few of my sermons that I copied and pasted from my notes. They are exactly as they appear in my notes except for a few minor changes.

I usually highlight my scripture verses in a medium blue font. It helps me recognize them quickly on the page as I'm working my way through the sermon. I also highlight my illustrations in bright red. That also helps me see them quickly and recognize them on the page.

I don't worry too much about everything being exactly aesthetically perfect on the pages. I'm normally the only one who will see them so I thought it important show them to you as as I preached them.

Feel free use any and all of them.

The Bible: God's Perfect Word

2 Timothy 3:14-17

14 But as for you, continue in what you have learned and have firmly believed, knowing from whom you learned it **15** and how from childhood you have been acquainted with the sacred writings, which are able to make you wise for salvation through faith in Christ Jesus. **16** All Scripture is breathed out by God and profitable for teaching, for reproof, for correction, and for training in righteousness, **17** that the man of God may be complete, equipped for every good work.

THE BIBLE IS PERFECT

Cottage Cheese and Vanilla Ice Cream

Series Intro: We are here today because we believe the Bible. We believe in the God of the Bible; the Christ of the Bible; the plan of salvation revealed in the Bible; and everything else written in the Bible.

"This book is the Word of God! I believe it is true from cover to cover. It is without error and it is absolutely perfect."

Sermon Intro: A good word that describes the Bible is the word *"unique"*. The dictionary defines the word *"unique"* as, *"being the only one of its kind, better than others: superior to all others.* It is the only book of its kind in existence! Several things point out the uniqueness of the Bible.

- The Bible was written over a period of **1,500 years**

- The Bible was written by over **40 different authors** (Among them were kings, military leaders, peasants, philosophers, fishermen, tax collectors, poets, statesmen, musicians, scholars and shepherds.)

- The Bible was written in **many different places, at many different times and by people experiencing many different moods**.

- The Bible was written on three continents: **Asia, Africa and Europe**.

- The Bible was written in three different languages: **Hebrew, Greek and Aramaic**.

- The Bible is written with many different literary styles: **Prose, poetry, historical narrative, romance, law, biography, parable, allegory and prophecy**.

- The Bible deals with hundreds of difficult issues without a single contradiction.

- The Bible is a book of great diversity, yet, in spite of this, it tells a single continuous story, and it does so without ever contradicting itself.

- The Bible's main character is God Himself, is made known through the person of His Son, the Lord Jesus Christ.

Yes, the Bible is a unique book! But, this uniqueness was not accidental, it was purposeful. How can this be? The Bible achieves its uniqueness through a process known as Inspiration. It is that process that I would like for us to investigate together today. Our text, **verse 16**, says that "***All scripture is given by inspiration of God***". The word "***inspiration***" literally means "***God breathed***".

If God has given His Word, delivered by His very breath, then it stands to reason that the scripture He has given us is absolutely perfect. Let's look into the matter of inspiration and think together for a while about ***The Perfection Of The Holy Scriptures***.

I. <u>THE PROCESS OF BIBLICAL INSPIRATION</u>

(Ill. What process did God use to get His Word into the hands and hearts of men? There are three terms that must be addressed as we deal with this matter of Inspiration.)

A. <u>Revelation</u> - The first step in getting the word of God on paper is the process known as revelation. This is the process whereby a man hears from the Lord just what the Lord wants written down. At varying times, God used varying means to give His revelation to men.

- He spoke through **<u>angels</u>** - **Gen. 18; 19; Luke 1-2; Matt. 28; etc.**

- He spoke through **<u>an audible voice</u>** - **Gen. 3:9-19; 6:13-21; 12:1-3; Ex. 20:1-17; Josh. 1:1-9; 1 Kings 17:2-4.**

- He spoke in a **still, small voice** - **1 Kings 19:11-12**

- He spoke through **nature** - **Psalm 19**

- He spoke through **animals** - **Num. 22:28**

- He spoke in **dreams** - **Gen. 28:12; Matt. 1-2; Matt. 2:19-22**

- He spoke through **visions** - **Isaiah 6:1-6; Daniel 7; 8; 10; Acts 16, 19**

- He spoke through **Christophanies** – **Gen. 18:1-33; Ex. 3:2; Dan. 3:25; 1 Kings 19:7**

We do not know the exact process by which God spoke to the original authors, but we have God's Word on the fact that He did, **2 Pet. 1:21, "For the prophecy came not in old time by the will of man: but holy men of God spake as they were moved by the Holy Ghost."** So, revelation is God telling a man what He wants written down.

B. **Inspiration** - The second step in the process is inspiration. This is man writing on paper what God has told him to say. As we have already seen this process is said to be "**God breathed**".

- The Bible clearly claims inspiration for itself, **2 Tim. 3:17; 2 Pet. 1:20-21; Heb. 1:1**.

- Paul believed his writings were inspired, **1**

Cor. 4:2; 15:3; 1 Thes. 2:13; 4:15.

· Peter believed his writings were inspired, **2 Pet. 3:2**.

· Peter believed the writings of Paul to be inspired, **2 Pet. 3:15-16**.

Somehow God superintended the process of getting His word into a man and then through that man onto paper. Inspiration has been defined as, "***God's superintendence of the human authors so that, using their own individual personalities, they composed and recorded without error His revelation to man in the words of the original autographs***", Charles C. Ryrie.

But, the question comes, how did He do this? Well, of course, there are many different views, but only one correct view.

Allow me to share with you the biblical view of inspiration. Most fundamentalists believe in what is called the "***Plenary, Verbal Inspiration of the Bible.***"

God gave His Word to human authors. But, He did not override their personalities. He did, however, guide their choice of words. When they had written down all that God had given them in His revelation, they had produced a perfectly inspired record of God's revelation. God breathed His Word through human vessels giving the world a perfectly inspired statement of His Word to men!

C. **Illumination** - The third process is getting the Word of God to men is the process known as illumination. This is "***the process by which God uses the inspired written record of His revelation to speak to the hearts of individual people.***" This is when the Holy Spirit causes the light to come on in the human heart and men see themselves as they are and Jesus as the need of their heart. It is also the process whereby the Spirit of God allows us to understand the truth of the Word of God. Thus, the cycle of inspiration is complete. Since inspiration is our topic this evening, we will leave the subject of illumination until a later time.

II.   **THE PROOF OF BIBLICAL INSPIRATION**

(Ill. Now that we have something of an idea of what inspiration is, how can we be sure that God genuinely inspires our Bibles?

Well, the bottom line is that it does come down to faith, but faith is never a blind leap into the dark. Our faith can rest not just in the fact that God personally breathed His Word through men, but that His Word will stand up to several important tests as to its perfection. Let me share a few of those with you.)

A. **It Passes The Historical/Archeological Test** - For many years people laughed at Bible believers because the Bible referred to places, people and events that had no basis in recorded history. However, through the good grace of

God, He has allowed the archeologists' spade to uncover many items from the ancient past that confirm the factual nature of the Word of God. Not a single piece of evidence had ever surfaced that contradicts the Bible at only point of its history.

(**Note**: Consider these important discoveries:

· For years men said that a place called Ur of the Chaldees never existed. Then proof was discovered that proved it did.

· The historicity of Joseph's rule in Egypt confirmed by a tablet found in Yemen. It seems that a clay tablet was found in the tomb of a rich woman who record here efforts to buy grain from a man named Joseph in a land called Egypt.

· The seal of Baruch, Jeremiah's scribe has been found.

· Jezebel's makeup saucers have been found.

· Brick in Egypt have been found that were made without straw.

· The death of Jesus has been proven to be a historical fact.

· The list could go on for hours, but suffice it to say that the Bible has been and continues to be proven accurate in every detail it records!)

(**Note**: This kind of accuracy is something else that no other religious text in existence can claim. Ill. ***The Book of Mormon***!) ***The Bible can be trusted!***

B. **It Passes The Scientific Test** - Others have mocked the Bible and claimed that it was woefully inaccurate in matters of science. However, time has once again vindicated the accuracy of the message of the Bible.

  · The Bible says the earth is a sphere, **Isa. 40:22**. Man discovered this in the 15th century.

  · The Bible says the earth is suspended in space - **Job 26:7**. Sir Isaac Newton discovered this in 1687.

  · The Bible claims the number of the stars is innumerable, **Gen. 15:5**. Abraham could only see about 1,200 stars in his day. Now, we know that there are trillions of stars in the heavens.

  · The Bible contains rules regarding medicine and sanitation that where thousands of years ahead of their time. (Ill. Washing and quarantine)

· Many, many more specific items could be mentioned here, but these should suffice to show the superiority of the message of the Bible.

The Bible can be trusted!

C. **It Passes The Prophecy Test** - There are literally thousands of prophetic predictions made in the Bible. Some of these prophecies are quite dramatic in nature. For instance, Isaiah mentions Cyrus the Persian King, by name, 125 years before he was born.

Not a single one prophecy made in the Bible has ever failed, or will ever fail, to come to pass! Some of the most remarkable prophecies are those related to the Lord Jesus Christ.

For instance, if you were to take just a few of the most specific prophecies concerning the Lord Jesus and His birth and earthly life, you can see how astonishing the accuracy of the Bible truly is. Consider just these seventeen prophecies:

1. He would be born in Bethlehem, **Micah 5:2**

2. He would be preceded by a forerunner, **Isa. 40:3**

3. He would enter Jerusalem on a colt, **Zech. 9:9** (By the way, Jesus entered Jerusalem on the exact day Daniel had prophesied hundreds of years earlier, **Dan. 9:25-27**.)

4. He would be betrayed by a friend, **Psa.**

41:9

5. His hands and His feet would be pierced, **Psa. 22:16**

6. He would be wounded by His enemies, **Isa. 53:5**

7. He would be betrayed for 30 pieces of silver, **Zech. 11:12**

8. He would be spit upon and beaten, **Isa. 50:6**

9. The betrayal money would be cast down in temple and would be used to buy a potter's field, **Zech. 11:13**

10. He would be silent before His accusers, **Isa. 53:7**

11. He would be crucified with thieves, **Isa. 53:12**

12. People would gamble for His garments, **Psa. 22:8**

13. His side would be pierced, **Zech. 12:10**

14. No a bone in His body would be broken, **Psa. 34:20**

15. His body would not decay, **Psa. 16:10**

16. He would be burial in the tomb of a rich man, **Isa. 53:9**

17. Darkness would cover the earth, **Amos 8:9**.

Someone has calculated that the odds of just these seventeen prophecies coming to pass is *1 chance in 480 Billion X 1 Billion X 1 Trillion*! That is **the number 480 followed by 30 zeros**!

In other words, it would be like taking one grain of sand, painting it gold, and hiding it somewhere among the 200 million stars and the millions of planets, moons and asteroids of the Milky Way, then blindfolding a person and sending him out to find that one golden grain of sand. The odds are the same that he would find it!

Even if you just take eight of the prophecies that refer to Jesus, it can be illustrated by the following. Suppose we filled the entire state of Texas two feet deep with silver dollars. We marked one with an "X" and stirred up all the silver dollars throughout the state. Then, we blindfolded a man and allowed him to go anywhere he wishes in the state of Texas, stop, reach down into the silver dollars and pick one out. *The odds that he would find the one marked silver dollar are 1 in 1017, or one in one hundred quadrillion, or one in 100 million billion.* Those are the odds!)

The Bible can be trusted!

D. **It Passes The Unity Test** - What God begins in Genesis, He ends in Revelation. (Ill. **Gen. 1:1; Rev. 21:1; Gen. 1:27-28; Rev. 21:9,** etc.) This is in spite of the fact that it took 1,500 years to write the Bible. It is the unfolding of a single story from beginning to end. This could never be duplicated by any human work!

The Bible can be trusted!

E. **It Passes The Honesty Test** - If this were merely a human book, it would gloss over the failures of the people found within its pages. However, the Bible does not hide Noah's drunkenness, Samson's lust, David's adultery, Elijah's depression or Peter's denial. It tells the truth from cover to cover!

The Bible can be trusted!

There are many other areas in which the Bible could be put to the test, but I just want you to know that it passes them all with flying colors! No human book could accomplish this! Just what I have mentioned this evening is proof positive that we have in our hands a divinely inspired Bible!

III. **THE PRODUCT OF BIBLICAL INSPIRATION**

(Ill. We know what inspiration is and we can see the God's fingerprints all over His Word. If we accept the Bible as the inspired Word of God, what does that teach us? What can we take away from such an examination? We are left with three precious truths that must never be taken for granted.)

A. **The Bible Is Infallible** - This word means that the Scriptures are incapable of failing! Everything the Bible says is truth and all everything it promises will come to pass! The Scriptures are in every sense perfect and they are a perfect revelation of the mind of God to man!

B. **The Bible Is Inerrant** - E.J. Young defines inerrancy this way, "***By this word, we mean that the Scriptures possess the quality of freedom from all error. They are exempt from the liability to mistake, incapable of error. In all their teachings they are in perfect accord with the truth.***"

   When people say that the Bible contains mistakes and errors, they are calling the very character of God into question! We are told that God simply cannot tell a lie, **Heb. 6:18**. If He claimed inspiration for His Word, then that Word must be inerrant. If it isn't then God lied when He claimed to have inspired the original text.

C. **The Bible Is Complete** - When the apostle John laid down his pen at the close of the book of Revelation, the revelation in the Scriptures was perfect and fully complete. There has not been a single inspired word since that time and there never will be. God has finished His Scriptures and we hold in our hands the perfect and complete record of that revelation. If you lived 10,000 life times and read every book ever written and that would ever be written, you would never again encounter another book like the Bible. In fact, you would never again encounter any other Scripture. The Bible is complete!

(**Note**: The final analysis is this: when you read your Bible, you are reading the very words of God! You can base your faith upon it! You can trust your eternity to it. You can embrace its message knowing that it reveals the very mind of God to man! It cannot fail! It cannot err! It will never be corrected, updated or amended! It is complete and it is perfect!)

Cottage Cheese and Vanilla Ice Cream

Conc: I trust this hasn't been too academic. I hope this message has served to help to further anchor your faith in the blessed Word of God. I thank Him for His perfect Word! I am thankful that this book has revealed the sin of my heart and pointed out that I was headed to Hell! I am also thankful that God illuminated my heart to allow me to see not only myself and my need, but also Jesus Christ the solution to my problem.

There may be someone here that has never been saved. Jesus loves you my friend and He wants to reveal Himself to you. Won't you come to Him and be saved today? Others here are guilty of neglecting their Bibles. Won't you come and confess that to Him and begin a new love affair with the inspired Word of God? Others may like to just come and bow before Him and thank Him for His perfect Book!

HOW TO MAKE A GREAT CHURCH EVEN GREATER

2 Chronicles 7:14

Uncle Luke's Rifle

Intro: Our churches are great churches. They are shining lights in a dark world. They are great churches because they are built upon the solid foundations of the Word of God, the will of God and the ways of God. We have great churches because we are not ashamed of our past, our convictions, our worship, our standards or our Lord. Our churches are great because those who attend honor Jesus Christ.

Our churches are great because they are places where the Savior is exalted, the Saints are edified and Sinners are evangelized.

I've spoken in 38 states & over 400 churches. I can tell you what I've found: churches which are solid in doctrine, secure in direction and sold out in devotion. I found churches that are hungry, hopeful, healthy and happy. I found a people who were ready,

141

willing, and able to go where God wants to take them. I found a great church, made up of great people, serving a great God. I will say it again: OUR Churches are GREAT CHURCHES!

This evening, I want to preach to a great congregation from great passage of Scripture. I want to share a great thought that has gripped my heart in these days. I want you to know that as great as this church is, it can be even greater! This verse teaches us the simple steps that tell us *How To Make A Great Church Even Greater*.

(**Note**: The context of this verse relates to the dedication of the Temple under King Solomon. God has just finished demonstrating His acceptance of the new house of worship by sending fire down from Heaven to consume the sacrifice, which was upon the altar, **7:1**. He filled the Temple with His great glory, and the people worshiped their God with praises, humility, sacrifices and several days of celebration, **7:2-11**. Then, God comes to speak to Solomon, **7:12-22**. God tells Solomon that He will bless Israel if they will honor the Lord; but if they refuse, there will be serious consequences, **7:12, 19-22**. However, our text promises them that God will hear them, heal them and help them if they will return to Him in humble repentance. This great promise to Israel has a great message for us this evening. Let's examine its words and learn **How To Make A Great Church Even Greater**.)

Mink $1500, Mercedes $72,000, Beach Front Property $520,000 – whose Cell phone is this anyway?

I. 1ST Step- APPRECIATE OUR CONNECTION TO GOD

A. **It Is An Intimate Connection** – "*My people*" – God claims those who are in a faith relationship with Him, **Heb. 11:16**. He purchased them and He owns them, **1 Pet. 1:18-19; 1 Cor. 6:19-20**. There is an intimate relationship that is acknowledged here.

B. **It Is An Identifying Connection** – "*Called by My Name*" – These people who have been redeemed by the Lord are also identified with Him. They bear His name before a world that does not know Him. They are to live and conduct themselves like they are the children of God. That is the responsibility of every child of God, **1 John 2:6; 1 Pet. 2:21**.

The first step in making a great church even greater is for us to acknowledge our connection to the Heavenly Father.

Rick's Haircut...

II. 2nd Step - <u>ACCEPT THE CHALLENGE OF GOD</u>

A. **<u>It Is A Challenge to Be Dependent</u>** – "*Humble themselves and pray*" – In the context, Israel was to come to the place where they admitted that they could not help themselves out of their problems.

· **When we humble ourselves before Him, we are admitting that we have no faith in our own abilities.**

· **When we call on His name in prayer, we are proclaiming our faith in His ability.**

B. **<u>It Is A Challenge To Be Devoted</u>** – "*Seek my face*" – This expression is translated form words which mean, "*To seek to find;* These words imply "*a* *yearning, a frequency of inquiry, a desire to enter into the presence of someone!"*

Not only are we to humble ourselves before Him, but also we are to live our lives with a hunger for Him!

·   **Paul** - *"That I may know him, and the power of his resurrection, and the fellowship of his sufferings, being made conformable unto his death;"* **Philippians 3:10**.

·   **David** – *"One thing have I desired of the LORD, that will I seek after; that I may dwell in the house of the LORD all the days of my life, to behold the beauty of the LORD, and to enquire in his temple."* **Psalm 27:4**.

C.   **It Is A Challenge To Be Different** – *"Turn from their wicked ways"* – It is a challenge for the people of God to live clean and holy lives for the glory of the Lord. The people of Israel are told to *"turn from their wicked ways."*

·   Money or Job, Possessions, Position or Status,   Pride and Hypocrisy, A relationship or a person,   Sexual immorality or Lust, Cheating or stealing,   Hobby or a Habit,

50-yard line, Seat at Sup Bowl. They're all at the funeral

III. Step 3 -   <u>ANTICIPATE THE CONFIRMATION FROM GOD</u>

A.   <u>He Will Hear Us</u> – "*Then will I hear from Heaven*" – When we, God's people, deal with this "*if*" situation; we are assured that God will hear us.   We all   know   that   sin   terminates   the   lines   of communication between the believer and the Lord, **Psa. 66:18**

B.   <u>He Will Help Us</u> – "*Will forgive their sin, and heal their land*" – When we pay the price to honor our relationship to the Lord and accept His challenge to a dependent, devoted and different life; He will hear our prayers, forgive our sins and heal our land.

In other words, when we come clean with the Lord and we meet His expectations, He will bless us with His power, honor us with His greatness and thrill us with His glory.   When we find that place before Him

146

that honors Him, we will see Him take a great church and make it even greater!

D.   Whenever you are turning away "*from*" one thing, you are naturally turning "*to*" some other thing.

(Ill. Here is what you need to do. You and I need to search our hearts and lives to see if there are any "*Idols there, which are leading us into sin*"? Here is a partial list:

Uncle Luke's Rifle

Preached at Victory FWB Church, Springfield TN

Rejoice FWB Church, Nashville, TN

A CLEAR MESSAGE
TO A CALLED MAN

2 Timothy 4:1-5

4 I charge you in the presence of God and of Christ Jesus, who is to judge the living and the dead, and by his appearing and his kingdom: **2** preach the word; be ready in season and out of season; reprove, rebuke, and exhort, with complete patience and teaching. **3** For the time is coming when people will not endure sound[a] teaching, but having itching ears they will accumulate for themselves teachers to suit their own passions, **4** and will turn away from listening to the truth and wander off into myths. **5** As for you, always be sober-minded, endure suffering, do the work of an evangelist, fulfill your ministry.

Mistaken Man

Jones was just 24 years old when he was convicted of trying to steal a woman's purse in the parking lot of a Wal-Mart in Roeland Park, the ABC reports. He was given the lengthy sentence despite having an alibi and despite the fact that no fingerprints or DNA evidence ever linked him to the crime.

His conviction was based on two flawed eyewitness accounts, according to the WASHINGTON POST.

The victim described her attacker as a thin, light-skinned man black or Hispanic man with dark hair and a police photo line-up showed Jones alongside five dark-skinned, black men.

After more than a decade of failed appeals, Jones learned that a man named Ricky Amos was also an inmate at the Lansing Correctional Facility. Jones then told staff at the Midwest Innocence Project and the University of Kansas School of Law that he was often mistaken for the man he'd never met.

"It made a lot of things understandable for me concerning this whole case," Jones told ABC. "I just looked at how much me and this man looked alike and it was unbelievable."

Intro: In our text, Paul is writing to a young preacher named Timothy whom Paul had ordained to preach the Gospel, **1 Tim. 4:14**. Paul knows that his time on this earth is short. Before he leaves this world, he wants Timothy to have a good understanding of what his calling and ministry are all about. Paul takes pen in hand and writes the verses we have as our text today. Paul issues *A Clear Message To A Called Man*.

Allow me to share some of the *aspects* of the preacher's call and ministry as they are presented in this passage. I want to preach on the subject: *A Clear Message To A Called Man*.

I. v. 1-2a <u>THE PREACHER'S MANDATE</u>

A. v. 2a <u>He Is To Be A Man Of The Word</u> –

Preach the Word – *Preach* = "*To herald*"
Refers to a king's messenger to the people. He was to sound out the king's word with a voice that was loud and clear. The message was to be heard and heeded. The messenger was to be respected and unhindered. He was not an ambassador with whom one might negotiate. He was a messenger that must be heard!

"*The Word*" refers to the whole counsel of the Bible, **Acts. 20:27**. The preacher's mandate is to be a man of the Word. Not of human philosophy and psychology; not of human wisdom and education; but of the unsearchable riches of Christ. The message is to be the Word of God alone!

This will require much study, **2 Tim. 2:15**. In fact, the preacher's life is to be a lifetime of commitment to the study of the Word of God.

Nothing will take the place of the preaching of the Word of God!

Nothing will ever replace preaching! It is the means God has chosen to save the world, **1 Cor. 1:21**. After 45 plus years of preaching I can testify to that!

B. v. 2a <u>He Is To Be A Master Of The Winds</u> –

Be instant – The word "*instant*" has the idea of "*being present, or being ready.*" The idea here is that there will be times when preaching is easy and times when it is hard. There will be times when you can't wait to get up there and preach and there will be times when just the thought of preaching will make you feel sick. There will be times when the people are listening and when they are turning a deaf ear to the message. ***Regardless of how the wind may be blowing at a particular time, the preacher is to stand forth and preach the Word of God.***

Be ready, be in your place and preach! No excuses, no whining, just a heart that is ready when the preaching moment presents itself.

C. v. 1 **He Is To Be Mindful Of The Witnesses** – ***Charge before God*** – Timothy is reminded that God and Jesus are observing the ministry of the preacher. He is also reminded that one day the preacher will give account to the Lord Jesus for the ministry he has performed, **2 Cor. 5:10; Rom. 14:12**.

II. v. 2b - 4 **THE PREACHER'S MESSAGE**

A. **It Must Be A Convicting Message** – ***Reprove*** – This is a word that refers to *preaching that brings conviction*. This has in mind preaching that corrects the errors of men's beliefs and practices.

This kind of preaching holds the bright light of the Word against the blackness of sin, thus exposing it for what it is!

152

Genuine biblical preaching exposes evil and brings conviction on sinners.

The true preacher will expose sin as he carefully preaches the Word of God.

B. **It Must Be A Confronting Message** – **Rebuke** – While a "***reproof***" exposes the sinfulness of sin; a "***rebuke***" exposes the sinfulness of the sinner.

This is the personal side of preaching. Sin must be confronted before sinners will be convicted!

God will use your preaching to confront sinners, if you preach the "***whole counsel of God.***"

Our preaching must warn the sinner of the dangers of his sin.

C. **It Must Be A Comforting Message** – **Exhort** - ***To call to one's side*** - When we preach, we are to *thunder against sin*, but we are also *to encourage and comfort* the people of God.

We don't do this with our intellect, or by our eloquent words of wisdom; rather, we do it by taking the Word for God and *showing His people a Biblical solution to their problems*.

Then, we aid them as they implement God's plan into their lives.

D. **It Must Be A Compassionate Message** –

Longsuffering – This word has the idea of "***patience, endurance***." As the preacher carries out his God-given ministry to confront sin, challenge the saints and comfort the hurting; he must always *keep in mind* that *he is still one of them*.

He is to walk with the people with the heart of a brother in Christ. We are to love them like the Lord loves them, "**charity suffereth long, and is kind**" **1 Cor. 13:4**.

E. **It Must Be A Confirming Message** –
   Doctrine – Paul returns to where he began: the Word of God. Here is where everything rises or falls.

We are to preach this Word and we are to instruct people in the doctrines of this book.

Your opinions, your beliefs, your thoughts are irrelevant! What matters is what "***thus saith the Lord!***"

The Bible is our sole authority! It tells people how to live and how to grow.

It teaches them how they are to respond to the reproofs and the rebukes of preaching.

It must never be compromised, but it must be proclaimed in power and heart-rending authority!

When it is, the Holy Spirit will take it and use it to illuminate the minds of people.

He will draw men to Himself the preaching of the trust of the Word of God!

III. **v. 5** **THE PREACHER'S MINISTRY**

A. **It Must Be A Ministry Of *Sobriety* – *Watch* –** It is a call for the man of God "***to be alert.***" Walk through life with your eyes open.

What is the preacher to watch for? He is to watch for the wolves that would destroy the flock, **Acts 20:28-30**.

He is to watch for the wicked one who would destroy his ministry, **1 Pet. 5:8**.

Many men have failed to watch and they have seen their ministries destroyed from within by sin and from without by invading wolves.

Watch, preacher watch!

B. **It Must Be A Ministry Of *Steadfastness* – *Endure* –** Serving God is not the easiest life in the world.

The enemies of the soul, the world, the flesh and the devil, are all striving to destroy you.

Add to that the fact that God often uses hardship to train us, (Ill. Elijah – **1 Kings 17**), and you will soon discover that "***hardship***" is part and parcel of the ministry!

———

The afflictions of life help us to comfort others when they are afflicted. (Ill. **Job 2:8** – It often takes someone that has been broken to minister to another who is broken.)

So, don't be surprised and fall out when the trials of life come your way!

It has been said that "***those God would use greatly, He first hurts deeply.***" I have found that to be true!

C. **It Must Be A Ministry Of *Sharing*** –
Evangelize – While the Lord may not have called you to a ministry of full-time evangelism; He has called you to evangelize.

The idea here is that pointing men to Jesus is at the heart of all we do.

The goal of every part of our ministry and the goal of every sermon should be to point men to the Lord Jesus Christ!

Whether you are in the pulpit or out, you are to be striving to bring people to the Master.

D. **It Must Be A Ministry Of *Stability*** – **Make Full Proof** – This word means "***to being in a full measure***." It was used regarding a ship moving across the sea with its sails set, catching every ounce of the available breeze!

The preacher is to set his sails, catch the wind of God and allow Him to use you to your fullest capacity.

156

Let nothing hold you back, but go with God! This will mean living the right kind of life. It will mean fulfilling the requirements of **1 Tim. 3:1-7, 11**.

It will mean that you need to be a man of God in the church, at home and in the public arena

Conc: Read again **2 Tim. 4:1-3, 5**. I challenge you to remember this charge and I pray that you will be blessed with a long, fruitful ministry for the glory of God!

Mistaken Man

A Missouri man is free after serving 17 years in prison in what officials think was a case of mistaken identity.

Richard Jones, 41, was exonerated and released on June 8 after serving a majority of his 19-year sentence for aggravated robbery in Kansas City. Jones learned that a man who may have been the true culprit was in the same prison — and realized the man looks just like him, **ABC News reports**.

"I hope and prayed every day for this day to come," Jones told ABC. "When it finally got here, it was an overwhelming feeling."

Coping With Criticism

Exodus 18:13-27

Built first building in Ahoskie, NC, Alton Raines

Criticism will come: A Fact of Life, Friend or Foe

- If you do anything.

- If you do nothing.

- After a great development in your life.

- After a great disappointment.

What are you doing? Do you know what you are doing< Moses – Great victory in chapter 17 against the Amalekites. Jethro hears things are going well. (Moses probably sent for his wife and children.

What should you do when you receive Criticism?

Remember the 4 L's...

The Auditor's Bank Robbery A story is told of two men who worked in the audit department of a large bank. They made an overnight trip to a distant branch of the bank, and were dining in a local restaurant. The chief auditor told the other man, "First we'll hit the tellers, and then get the vault." They arrived at the bank the next morning, only to be promptly arrested by the state police. Upon inquiry, they discovered that a police captain had eaten at the same restaurant and had overheard the conversation about "hitting the tellers and getting the vault." The police captain had made a very good assumption about the situation, based on the information as he had overheard it, but his assumption was also very wrong.

I. 1st Listen to it. 18:14-23

A. The Problem **17-18- Ex 18:17 Moses' father-in-law replied, "What you are doing is not good. 18 You and these people who come to you will only wear yourselves out. The work is too heavy for you; you cannot handle it alone.**

B. The Purpose **19-20 - Ex 18:19 Listen now to me and I will give you some advice, and may God be with you. You must be the people's representative before God and bring their disputes to him. 20 Teach them the decrees and laws, and show them the way to live and the duties they are to perform.**

C. The Plan **21-23- Ex 18:21 But select capable men from all the people-- men who fear God, trustworthy men** who hate dishonest gain-- and appoint them as officials over thousands, hundreds, fifties and tens. 22 Have them serve as judges for the people at all times, but have them brought every difficult case to you; the simple cases they can decide themselves. That will make your load lighter, because they will share it with you. 23 If you do this and God so commands, you will be able to stand the strain, and all these people will go home satisfied."

Radio- Pulled off knobs. The story is told of a man who once bought a new radio, brought it home, and placed it on the refrigerator. He then plugged it in, turned it to WSM in Nashville (home of the Grand Ole Opry), and proceeded to do the most unusual thing. He pulled all the knobs off! He had already tuned in all he ever wanted or expected to hear, and so he chose to limit his radio reception to one station.

II. Look at it. Verse 24 - Ex 18:24 Moses listened to his father-in-law and did everything he said.

A. The Criticism was Presented Accurately. (Jethro was right)

III. Learn from it. Verses 25-26 - Ex 18:25 He chose capable men from all Israel and made them leaders of the people, officials over thousands, hundreds, fifties and tens. 26 They served as judges for the people at all times. The difficult cases they brought to Moses, but the simple ones they decided themselves.

   A. The Plan was adopted.

   B. The Plan was implemented

   C. The Plan was successful

One Talent Man – Criticism A guy came to his pastor and said, "Reverend, I only have one talent."

The pastor asked, "What's your talent?

The man said, "I have the gift of criticism."

The pastor was wise and replied, "The Bible says that the guy who had only one talent went out and buried it. Maybe that's what you ought to do with yours."

IV. Live above it.

   A. Listened to it.

   B. Looked at it.

C. Learned from it.

If the criticism is not warranted, just live above it. Move on with your life and ministry.

Built first building in Ahoskie, NC, Alton Raines